MAKE ROOM FOR Daddy

Resources from MOPS

Books
Beyond Macaroni and Cheese
Children Change a Marriage
A Cure for the Growly Bugs
  and Other Tips for Moms
Getting Out of Your Kids' Faces
  and Into Their Hearts
In the Wee Hours
Loving and Letting Go
Mom to Mom
Meditations for Mothers
A Mother's Footprints of Faith
Ready for Kindergarten
What Every Child Needs
What Every Mom Needs
When Husband and Wife
  Become Mom and Dad

Little Books for Busy Moms Series
Boredom Busters
Great Books to Read and Fun
  Things to Do with Them
If You Ever Needed Friends,
  It's Now
Juggling Tasks, Tots, and Time
Kids' Stuff and What to Do
  with It
Planes, Trains, and Automobiles
  ... with Kids!
Time Out for Mom . . . Ahhh
  Moments

Books with Drs. Henry Cloud
and John Townsend
Raising Great Kids

Raising Great Kids for Parents
  of Preschoolers Workbook
Raising Great Kids for Parents
  of Teenagers Workbook
Raising Great Kids for Parents
  of School-Age Children
  Workbook

Gift Books
God's Words of Life from
  the Mom's Devotional Bible
Mommy, I Love You Just
  Because

Kids Books
Little Jesus, Little Me
My Busy, Busy Day
See the Country, See the City
Mommy, May I Hug the Fishes?
Mad Maddie Maxwell
Zachary's Zoo
Morning, Mr. Ted
Boxes, Boxes Everywhere
Snug as a Bug?

Bible
Mom's Devotional Bible

Audio
Raising Great Kids

Curriculum
Raising Great Kids for
  Parents of Preschoolers
  ZondervanGroupware™
  (with Drs. Henry Cloud
  and John Townsend)

MOTHERS OF
M♥PS.
PRESCHOOLERS

...because mothering matters

MAKE ROOM FOR Daddy

A Mom's Guide to Letting Dad Be Dad

Elisa Morgan & Carol Kuykendall

Foreword by Dr. Henry Cloud and Dr. John Townsend

ZONDERVAN™

GRAND RAPIDS, MICHIGAN 49530

We want to hear from you. Please send your comments about this book to us in care of the address below. Thank you.

GRAND RAPIDS, MICHIGAN 49530

WWW.ZONDERVAN.COM

ZONDERVAN™

Make Room for Daddy
Copyright © 2002 by Elisa Morgan and Carol Kuykendall

Requests for information should be addressed to:
Zondervan, *Grand Rapids, Michigan 49530*

ISBN 0-310-24044-1

Published in association with the literary agency of Alive Communications, Inc., 7680 Goddard Street, Suite 200, Colorado Springs, CO 80920.

Interior design by Todd Sprague

Printed in the United States of America

02 03 04 05 06 07 08 /❖ DC/ 10 9 8 7 6 5 4 3 2 1

*To the moms who shape the offerings
of their children's fathers*

Contents

Foreword

If you're a mom, you want what's best for your child. A major part of that is in how he or she is fathered, because fathering is key to a child's development. The primary goal of parenting is to produce a healthy adult who is able to meet life's demands, and that task ideally requires the input and resources of both a father and a mother.

With this in mind, Elisa and Carol have written a very significant book that looks at the fathering role and provides mothers with a unique approach to assisting her child's father in his growth and development as a dad.

This approach is helpful for several reasons. First, your ultimate concern is the personal and spiritual growth of your child. Though the word *child* is not in the title, *Make Room for Daddy* is really about your child. The more parents are partners in the process, the more children benefit,

9

because God's plan is for kids to be parented by both mom and dad.

Second, moms are often more aware of the child's need for an active and competent dad than fathers are themselves. With his own demands and life responsibilities, a dad sometimes isn't as in touch with these needs as a mom is. As husbands and fathers ourselves, we have often personally experienced the benefits of wives who point out some way we could be helpfully involved in parenting we hadn't even thought of.

Third, the book provides many ways a mom can help dad be a better dad, without running the risk of being controlling or of mothering him. Your child needs two grownups, not a mom and an extra big brother! Elisa and Carol do a great job of giving an approach that preserves the adulthood of both mom and dad, while allowing mom to influence in loving and respectful ways.

A unique advantage of *Make Room for Daddy* is also in how it treats gender differences. We believe that, in many ways, men and women are certainly not the same; yet the sexes are ultimately more alike than they are different. So in good parenting, your child is helped more when both parents take on the tasks of loving, connecting emotionally, providing structure, disciplining, and giving spiritual nourishment. Though moms and dads have their specialty areas, there is a great deal of overlap.

Mom, you may be overwhelmed with the prospect of adding "help him be a dad" to your long to-do list. It certainly can be a lot of extra work. But we men are trainable! Look at it as the kind of work that, the sooner you undertake it, the greater its rewards for all of you. When you take on the task of assisting your child's father in finding his way as a dad, you invest in a solid foundation for the future—a foundation that will bear many blessings in your child's life. Not only this, but for those of you who are married, *Make Room for Daddy* will help you put a lot of your values and interests in one place, as these ideas all come together. A better dad is a better husband, and a better husband is a better man. Your child, your husband, your marriage, and your soul are all nourished and strengthened. So get to work on the book! Most likely, a good dad is waiting to become a great dad!

Elisa and Carol have done a great service here. We are thankful for their lives. And we pray God's best in your own life as you parent.

—Dr. Henry Cloud and Dr. John Townsend

Acknowledgments

For many years, we've been gathering thoughts and experiences for this book. Not only from our combined number of years of mothering and fathering with our husbands, but also from our combined years of working with thousands and thousands of mothers of young children through MOPS International. This book looks at the process of growing as moms and dads, and our desire to help moms understand how much they influence the fathers of their children in their efforts to be good dads. We have many people to thank who helped us translate thoughts and ideas into words and onto the pages that make up this book.

First, thanks to all the moms and dads (more than a thousand!) who responded to our survey on the internet; for sharing your experiences and giving us your insights about this topic. Your honesty makes this book real.

Thanks also to Dr. Adrienne Ochs, a MOPS mom and researcher who helped us formulate and figure out the results of all those questionnaires.

We so appreciate Gail Burns, our faithful typist and foot-note-fixer-and-finder (big job!).

We are grateful for the loyalty and support and contributions of Mary Beth Lagerborg, our Publishing Director at MOPS International, our editor Sandy VanderZicht at Zondervan, and Rick Christian and Chip MacGregor of Alive Communications, for their advocacy of the mission of MOPS.

We save the best for last! We want to thank our husbands, Evan Morgan and Lynn Kuykendall, for their grace and love and incredible patience, because we've learned most of our lessons in the years we've spent mothering and fathering together. Despite our many less-than-perfect efforts, you've been great dads. Our love for each of you continues to grow!

About This Book

Welcome, mom! This book is about helping the father of your children be the best dad he can be—and your powerful influence in that process.

You may have picked this book up because you think your husband is a pretty good dad. He doesn't always do things exactly the way you do. He sometimes feeds the kids cake or cookies for breakfast (hey, they were *oatmeal* cookies!), lets them wear weird combinations of clothes (as if he doesn't even notice), and forgets about baths before bed. But you know he cares about being a good dad, and you want to partner with him in his efforts.

Maybe you're a bit disappointed that your husband isn't quite measuring up to what you hoped your children would have in a dad. He's too busy or preoccupied to sense their needs. He doesn't take the initiative; he always waits for you to tell him what to do. He doesn't care about the stuff you see as vital and sometimes he's too harsh in disciplining them.

Maybe you're a mom somewhere in between, just looking for ways to affirm your husband and encourage him to be a better dad. Or maybe you're not married to the father of your children, but you want your children to have the best of their dad, and you're committed to that effort.

In all these cases, this book is for you!

You might wonder why MOPS International is writing a book on fathering—after all, we're the experts on moms, not dads. At MOPS International (Mothers of Preschoolers), we work with millions of moms—some closely and others from a distance. The deepest longing we hear over and over again is that every mom wants to be the best mom possible. That means giving your child the best life possible. And that includes having a good dad.

In gathering information for this book, we did lots of research. We read books and articles, searched the web, and talked to experts. We also relied on our own personal experiences and the experience of working with MOPS moms all over the world. Probably most important, we pored over the results of our survey of more than a thousand moms and dads of young children. We asked dads such questions as: What is your description of a good dad? What do you need from your kids' mom to be a good dad? What does she do to encourage you to be a good dad? What discourages you?

We asked moms for descriptions of a good dad: What would make your husband a better dad? How can you encourage him to be a better dad? How important is fathering in the life of your child? Ninety-four percent of moms marked the highest ranking for their answer to this last question: "*Very important!*"

So we know you care about giving your children the best dad possible; we also know that you have an incredible amount of influence on what kind of daddy he will be. Ken Canfield, executive director of the National Center for Fathering, asked thousands of men, "Who has helped you the most in your fathering?" While some answered "my father" or "my pastor," the most frequent answer was "my wife," which led him to conclude that "beside every great dad is a great wife."[1]

In addition to compiling and including the answers to many of our survey questions, this book is based on these main principles:

- Our children need dads as well as moms.
- Moms and dads are different. A dad will love and parent his children differently from a mom. These differences are good, and children need both kinds of love as they grow up.
- Men want to be good dads just as women want to be good moms.
- As moms, we can influence our children's father in powerful ways by "making room for daddy."

The book is divided into three parts, "A New Style," "Mommy Style," and "Daddy Style." At the end of each chapter, you will find a section titled "Make Room for Reflection," which includes questions to think about on your own or in a small group. You will also find the section "Top Tips about Pops from MOPS," moms' helpful answers to some questions in our survey. One of the most important sections of the book is called "What to Do Next," a collection of how-to's or practical applications of the principles of this book. The topics covered by this section are listed at the back of the book in the "Quick Topic Finder" for your easy reference, and they are also flagged throughout the book, kind of like links on a web page. Also included in the "What to Do Next" section is a list of recommended resources for further reading.

Mom, you *can* make a difference in how well your husband fathers, and this book will tell you how. You'll discover there are some things you can stop doing as well as start doing. Don't be surprised if you find yourself growing in the process! Read on and learn how you can make room for daddy in the life of your child.

—Elisa Morgan
and Carol Kuykendall
for MOPS International

part one **A New Style**

chapter one

The Birth of a Father

It was about six o'clock on a summer evening, and she was busy browning ground meat for tacos. She lifted the lid and stirred seasoning into the stuff in the skillet. The screen door slammed for the umpteenth time that hour as another child raced through to the backyard, the dog following with eager barks.

With the back of her hand she brushed her forehead and turned down the heat on the stove. Too hot to cook. In the next room the older children were humming into the electric fan, forcing their voices into strange alien whines over the vibration of the blades. "Careful not to get too close to that fan!" she hollered, wiping her hands on a dishtowel.

Just then Dad burst through the kitchen door, slapping the screen back yet once more. A huge watermelon was tucked under his arm and an even huger grin spread across his face. "First watermelon of the season!" he announced. "Let's go on a watermelon picnic!"

All three kids squealed with delight at the prospect of such an adventure. She hesitated only for a moment, but in the next second her decision was made. Whatever. Forget dinner tonight.

"Great idea!" she responded, as she grabbed a blanket. In a few minutes the whole family had piled into the car and were on their way to their favorite park. They watched Dad take out his pocket knife and slice through the watermelon, which seemed to erupt with juice. Perched on a picnic table, legs dangling, they worked at their wedges while pausing now and then to spit the seeds at each other. Ah, the first watermelon of the summer.

Later that night as she tucked her youngest in bed, she touched his still-sticky hair. "Did you have fun tonight, pumpkin?" she asked.

His grin spread as wide as his father's had earlier in the evening. "Wow! Yes, Mom!" he said. "Isn't Dad the best dad in the world?" "Yes, son," she said, "he certainly is."

—**Charlene Ann Baumbich, "The Watermelon Picnic"**

When a child is born or adopted, a mother is born. That's become a familiar saying. But a father is born as well. In a miraculous moment, completely out of his control, a man becomes a father, and his whole life begins to change in ways he hadn't imagined.

Surprise! You're a Dad!

He thinks he's prepared. After all, he attended childbirth classes, learning how to be a coach and pant in unison with his wife. He's read all the recommended stuff. He's even reviewed his own childhood, thinking about the ways his parents raised him and deciding which patterns he wants to carry on and which ones he wants to change. For the last nine months he's tried to meet his wife's needs, offering back massages and trucking to the store to fulfill midnight food urges for peanut butter and pickle sandwiches. He's checked into health insurance and wills, put the crib together, and set up the nursery. He's even lain awake at night, nervously anticipating all the unknown responsibilities ahead of him.

And then suddenly he is born into the reality that he is, indeed, a brand-new dad. Now what?

Daddy Doubts

Most dads are surprised by the demands of their new role. Humorist Dave Barry describes his own new-fathering experiences like this:

When people ask me, "Dave, what's it like to have a newborn baby in the household?" I immediately answer: (nothing).

This is because I am sleeping. I spend a lot of my day in an unconscious state, because my 2-month-old daughter, Sophie, does not believe in sleeping at night. She feels that the nighttime hours are best used for making loud, inexplicable, Exorcist-style noises. At 3:30 A.M., her bassinet will suddenly start shaking like an unbalanced washing machine and erupt with a wide range of squeaks, gurgles, chirps, snorts, snuffles, grunts, etc. It does not sound like there's a lone baby in there. It sounds like the entire Barnyard of the Demons.[1]

Another new father writes, "When I brought home my daughter it was like, 'Here's the real world.' We went through Lamaze, the birth, but this [coming home] is when it hit: now there's a person who will be with us for the rest of our lives."[2]

Can you relate? The initiation of a man into fatherhood is like landing on a foreign planet. No wonder various "daddy doubts" emerge.

SEE "WHAT TO DO NEXT": HOW TO HELP HIM GET STARTED AS A DAD, PAGE 166.

"Let Me Catch Up with You!"

A woman who carries and delivers her child (rather than becomes a mom through adoption) has had a unique nine months to prepare physically and emotionally for the event of motherhood. Obviously her husband hasn't had the same experience, and though he's been more than involved in the process, his first real physical (and sometimes emotional) connection with the baby is *after* the birth. "Men and women during pregnancy are in the same stadium but on an entirely different playing field," says author Ian Davis. "After a testosterone-filled yell—'my boys can swim!'—it's time (for Dad) to go into a nine-month hibernation, only to be awakened when it's time to head off to the delivery room."[3]

The woman, on the other hand, becomes aware of her intimate physical connection to the baby the moment she passes the pregnancy test. She starts taking potent vitamins. She stops drinking coffee. She yearns for the first sensation of the baby moving within her, and then celebrates that flutter-feeling. In the last three months of her pregnancy, she eats like a weight lifter, walks like a rodeo cowboy, and sleeps little if at all while the baby takes over nearly *all* of her internal space. By the time she delivers, she may be relieved the whole two-for-one thing is over, but she's already developed an intimate bond with the child.

Dad has not had the same physical experience, and may recognize that he's getting a late start. "I have come to believe that by virtue of carrying and bearing these children, she can see things in them and about them that I tend to miss completely," Ken Canfield, head of the National Center for Fathering, writes about his wife. "The pain women have to endure in childbearing and the intensity of this experience make me believe they are much more tuned in to their children; they can tell things that fathers cannot."[4]

Others recognize that "fathers must continually work at developing and maintaining an emotional, intellectual, and physical connection to being a parent in this season in which their experience is so different from that of the mothers of their children. Generally speaking, it takes more effort for fathers to achieve than it does for mothers, since fathers-to-be are forever nine months behind in making this physical connection."[5]

For the father, the delivery of the child may mark the beginning of reality. As one father observed, "Watching my wife's belly move is in no way the same thing as holding a seven- or eight-pound infant."[6] The birth of a child may very well bring about confused, panicky feelings of, "Wait a second, I'm not up to speed yet! Let me catch up with you!"

"How Do You Do This?"

Dads desperately want to be there for their wives, the new mommies of their babies. Still, many get lost in their longing to help. In his book, *She's Had a Baby: And I'm Having a Meltdown*, James Douglas Barron describes his attempts to help on the day he brought his wife and new baby home from the hospital.

> After I helped my wife walk into the apartment, we stumbled around—strangers in a strange land. Finally, my wife plopped down on the living room couch. There was a millisecond of quiet. Then, everything happened at once. Our baby wailed piteously, my wife's breasts became clogged, and while I searched for the Extra Strength Tylenol, our phone began ringing off the hook with well-wishers and family. . . . I tried to calm our baby, called my wife's doctor, whipped up some lunch, and fell onto the couch beside my wife. Then, I started to laugh.
>
> Like every man in my shoes, I pondered the future, but became immediately aware that here it was, slamming through the walls of our living room like some runaway train. My eyes took in my desk, piled high with work and bills. Suddenly, I blurted out, "How are we going to do all this? The most I've ever cared for is a golden retriever!"[7]

Your husband may have a hard time dealing with the overwhelming details of caring for a new baby and a home. You've been trained to wake every hour because of your frequent urge to go to the bathroom during the last stage of pregnancy. He hasn't. Consequently, he doesn't automatically hear the baby's first cry and run to change the diaper as he promised. He catches on quickly though, taking to heart your complaints about being so tired.

By the third day home, he's worn out. Completely. He's trying to maintain normalcy around the house but didn't know you're supposed to cut bread with a serrated knife or it would turn into messy, crummy shreds. He had never heard of a "right" and "wrong" side for bedsheets. And his emotions soar and sink with yours. Attempts at romance fall short as you respond with glazed eyes, drugged moans, and a look that says, "If you touch me, you'll lose your life."

While he's conquered the laundry and the dishwasher, he's still having trouble keeping up with the sheer number of mismatched responsibilities falling to him. You overhear him mumbling something about multitasking, which is a good sign that he appreciates your abilities in a whole new way.

"Something Is Weird Here!"

A surefire surprise for every new father is witnessing the intimacy of the mother-infant bond. One dad commented that it was just plain *weird* to see a baby sucking at his wife's breast. His mind tells him this is normal, even fine. But something in his gut quirks at the image. Then there's the plastic bags of frozen breast milk he finds lodged next to the peas in the freezer every time he reaches for the carton of ice cream. He consoles himself with the realization that at least his wife's breast-feeding means he usually doesn't have to get up and deal with the baby's hunger in the "o-dark-thirty" hours of the night.

In some ways, he grieves the loss of the way things were, even though he can't identify his mixed-up feelings as those of grief. As excited as he is about the baby, he knows your marriage and your lives have changed forever. You don't have the same freedom you once enjoyed. The two of you can't be spontaneous about anything. Sometimes he forgets—and then remembers. *Oh, yeah. We can't go to a late movie on the spur of the moment.* Sometimes that forgetting, remembering, and then regretting is just plain *weird!*

"Where Do I Fit In?"

When he digs a bit deeper than his "this is weird" response, dad often faces a more honest and vulnerable question. He wonders, *Where do I fit in?* Sure, he's fallen in love with his new baby—a goofy goo-goo kind of love that he didn't know lived inside of him. He's not even embarrassed to coo in a silly, high-pitched baby-talk voice. He's proud. He's full of dreams for the future. Images of baseball games, piggyback rides and daddy-daughter outings swell his heart with a love that words don't describe.

But as he watches mother and baby together, he also struggles with feelings of trespassing, insignificance, and inadequacy. All those months he'd thought, *We're pregnant.* Now he wonders just what *we* means. Even when a child comes into a family through adoption, the bond between baby and mother in the early weeks is unsettling for many husbands. The space a husband used to occupy is suddenly filled as attention is totally given to the baby. Dads are left wandering about looking for ways to be helpful and wondering, *Just where do I fit in here?*

"Yikes! I'm a 'Dad'?"

Then there's the name change. The new identity. He's not just a guy or a husband. Now he's a dad. A *father.* That's way serious stuff. The weight of this new responsibility sinks in slowly. Gradually he realizes that he's responsible for money, safety, rules, and a ton of other stuff! He begins to wonder if he'll be able to handle the job description that goes along with his new title.

Robert Byron offers these "Random Thoughts from a Tired New Father": "I've been a father for about two weeks now and my son Malcolm is great; although his first week, he did get out of line. Messy diapers and crying about everything . . . he's such a baby. Sleep deprivation is the order of the day as Malcolm dictates the pattern of slumber. . . . I will say, however, that last night I slept like a baby. I cried all night and wet the bed."[8]

No doubt about it, becoming a father launches a new identity in the man you love. He's set out on a new adventure and will need to explore the person he is now becoming: dad!

SEE "WHAT TO DO NEXT": HOW TO HELP HIM FIND FRIENDS, PAGE 172.

"Will I Be a Good Dad?"

Fatherhood surprises and frightens most new dads. (Just as motherhood surprises and frightens us.) Men wonder, *Just what makes a good dad good?* and *Will I be a good dad? Do I have what it takes?* There's the fear of the unknown. Fear of making mistakes. Even fear of failing altogether. Dads think back to their own father's way of fathering, searching for clues for success. If they had good role models, they are encouraged, but often they find only more fears that they might unwittingly commit the same mistakes. In their very worst moments, they assign their mistrust of themselves to their wives, whom they previously saw as completely competent women. They wonder how a woman who locks herself out of her car or forgets to balance her checkbook can possibly handle the responsibility of being primary caretaker of his baby.

In his book *Don't Make Me Stop the Car! (Adventures in Fatherhood)*, *Today Show* host Al Roker writes of getting over those doubts that sometimes overwhelm dads in the beginning. "I think most of us are prewired to be parents," he says.

"For some of us the switch is hidden behind some sheetrock. But once you have the baby, that sheetrock comes off and you flip the switch, and you go 'Oooh, I love this!'"[9]

When dads have doubts, moms can go a long way to soothing those concerns, helping their husbands find the switch behind the sheetrock.

Make Room for Reflection

- Start by trying to walk around inside *his* heart. Try to feel his feelings and understand his doubts. Think about the questions he is asking: "How will I ever catch up with you?" "Where do I fit in?" "Can I handle all these new responsibilities?" "Will I be a good dad?" And perhaps most central to his concerns: "Just what *is* a good dad?"

- Help him identify his doubts and talk about them together. Most of all, love him through his doubts and let him know that you love him by what you say and what you do.

- If one of his doubts or fears grows out of the lack of a good model of fathering, encourage him to spend time with other dads. Women naturally join or form groups where they receive encouragement and share ideas, such as MOPS (Mothers of Preschoolers). Dads also need support and will benefit from sharing stories and ideas with other dads in a group from church, school, or neighborhood.

- Try to understand his fears. Some may make sense to you; others may be completely irrational, but are real to him. Here is James Barron's description of those fears:

Nine Things a New Father Fears Most about Fatherhood

1. No matter how hard I'll try to protect our baby, something will go wrong.
2. My wife loves our baby more than me.
3. Sex as I've known it is over.

4. Leisure time as I've known it is over.

5. Adventure as I've known it is over.

6. My youth as I've known it is over.

7. My wife will always be demanding, irritable, inconsolable, crazy, achy, tired, bad-mannered, and addicted to Extra Strength Tylenol.

8. I'll become a lethally dull, gin-and-tonic guzzling, work-complaining, short-fused, business-page-reading, pot-bellied paradigm of fatherhood.

9. I'll become divorced from my wife, fall for a bleached-blond second wife, wear a silver toupee and a navy blazer and gray slacks and loafers with gold bridle chains, see my kid on Wednesdays and every other weekend, and work at a job I hate—to pay the college tuition of a son who sides with his mother.[10]

Top Tips about Pops from MOPS

- I always find specific examples to describe how well he's doing.
- I left the bed this morning with our nine-month-old and my husband in it. The baby cried briefly, but soon they were giggling together.
- I encourage him that parenting is definitely a learn-as-you-go job.
- I told him, "You know, it's okay for you to nurture him," and it was like he was waiting for permission to do just that. From then on he was much more comforting and loving!
- I try to ask him for his opinion frequently ("Do you think I've dressed her warmly enough?" or "Honey, do you think she's hungry?"). Doing this seems to give him more confidence.

chapter two

Daddy Daze

What is a "good dad?"

We asked many moms, and here's what they said:

- He is a good provider, a strong and consistent disciplinarian, a role model, and someone to have a lot of fun with.
- He is both tough and tender and offers unconditional love at all times. He does not discipline out of anger, but out of love and always in the best interests of the child.
- He supports the mother, works as a team with her, and understands how difficult being a mom is.
- He spends time with his kids, shares fully in the responsibility of raising them, and is spiritually involved in their lives.
- He realizes when he makes mistakes, and he asks for forgiveness.
- He is loving, and his family always comes first. He is patient, calm, present, confident, comfortable, and silly. He does not have to be told what to do.

These composite descriptions came from moms who responded to our survey, but "good dad" descriptions are all around us—in words, in examples, and in the heart longings of our imaginations. "Good dads" show up in television shows, greeting card verses, newspaper articles, and cartoons. Some "good dads" sound more honest or humorous than others. Bill Cosby frequently quips that a good dad is one who pretends "the present you love best is soap on a rope."

A Picture of a Good Dad
(as drawn by moms)*

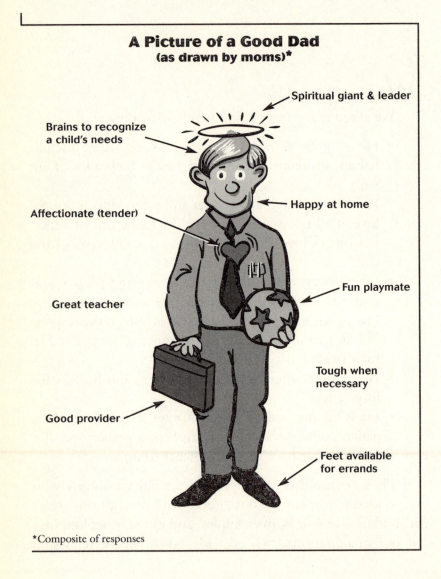

Spiritual giant & leader

Brains to recognize a child's needs

Happy at home

Affectionate (tender)

Fun playmate

Great teacher

Tough when necessary

Good provider

Feet available for errands

*Composite of responses

We Need Dads

If you look back over these descriptions, you realize that no dad measures up to all these "good dad" standards. But kids don't need perfect dads, nor do we need our husbands to be perfect dads. We all just need them to be dads! Plain and simple. And for their own sakes, dads need to *be* dads.

Kids Need Dads

In our survey, moms agreed that fathering is "very important" in the life of a child. Experts and research concur. A dad helps determine a child's success and happiness. A dad helps shape a child's confidence and emotional stability. He is a role model, positive or negative. He is crucial to the parenting process. A dad leaves an indelible thumbprint on the soul of a child. "Without my father it would be like a ball without any air inside it," a child writes.[1]

We have only to peek within the walls of our own hearts to validate the importance of fathering in the lives of children. How many of us carry painful holes left by our own fathers' failings? "By far the most issues adults bring into counseling are related directly with the father," says Dr. Frank Minirth. "If the father backs off—steps out of the picture—he exerts a tremendous negative impact."[2] The absence of a father causes a lifelong father wound and father hunger.

The importance of fathering is dramatically demonstrated by what happens when a father isn't around. Studies of fatherless children show that they are at risk in the following ways:

- They are more likely to score lower academically.
- They are more likely to drop out of high school.
- They are more likely to abuse drugs and alcohol.
- They are more likely to become involved in delinquent behaviors.[3]

Do sons and daughters need their dads equally? The answer is yes! When daughters hit early adulthood, they specifically benefit from their fathers' moral judgments and teachings from earlier in their lives.[4] Studies show that boys with dads who are intimately involved in their lives are more confident, adaptable, personable, and academically success-ful.[5] And it's common knowledge that sons learn how to treat females through the example of their fathers. Both genders gain an understanding of their sexuality from both father and mother.[6] Perhaps most astonishing is the faithlessness of fatherless children. The lack of a clear father figure is the most important ingredient in atheism and agnosticism.[7]

In spite of these findings, the world around us sometimes devalues the importance of a father, as one newspaper colum-nist lamented: "Somehow we have bought into a lie that says a father is dispensable, that anything he brings to the table can be replicated by a determined single mother or, indeed, any loving person who happens to be around. . . . Maybe it's a lie of necessity . . . but it's a lie, nonetheless. And it's past time we called it that."[8]

Kids need dads. And not just any dad will do. Kids need *their* dad. And they need him to be a good daddy.

Moms Need Dads to Be Dads

A mom needs her husband to be a dad because she wants what is best for her child. She also wants a partner in parent-ing who will share the responsibilities of raising children. In simple terms, the more he does, the less she has to do. But teamwork also brings the best results. Shared goals for expec-tations of behavior are easier to carry out and easier for a child to accept. When one parent loses patience or perspective, the other is there. When one feels confused about a plan of action, the other may have clarity. Teamwork also offers the best balance because a mom and dad offer different kinds of love, and a child needs both.

Therapist Erich Fromm says that a child from a balanced family receives two kinds of love. Mother-love tends to be unconditional, accepting the child no matter what, regardless of behavior. Father-love tends to be more provisional, bestowing approval as the child meets certain standards of behavior. Ideally, says Fromm, a child should receive and internalize both kinds of love.[9]

A father of young children validates Fromm's finding. "Our family needs both mom and dad in order to function properly," he writes. "In each of our strengths and weaknesses, we form a single complete team that is doing our best to show our children what it means to work together and support each other. Where I bring order, she brings warmth. Where I bring detail, she brings beauty. Where I bring discipline, she brings kindness."[10]

Dads Need to Be Dads

Dads benefit in immeasurable ways when they fulfill their role as fathers. Their investment in fathering gives their lives greater meaning and contributes to their sense of well-being. "Because his family is so much a part of him, he is actually investing in his own life both directly and indirectly," write the authors of *The Father Book*. "Certainly he invests materially with his paycheck. But when he makes a heavy relationship investment in addition, the chances of his marriage succeeding will go way up. The chances of his children succeeding will skyrocket. And as he leads his children spiritually, he grows spiritually himself. The father himself benefits, in every dimension."[11]

Defining Daddy

While the need for fathers in the lives of children has remained constant through the ages, the definition of what makes a good dad good has evolved through time in America, swinging from involvement to noninvolvement and back to involvement again through the decades of the past century. Another shift has occurred in the *recognition* of the importance of dad's involvement.

In the early 1900s, dads were very much involved around the home. Over half of America's population was rural, and dads worked side by side with their children. However, with the move to the urban world as a result of the industrial revolution, dads went off to work each day away from the home, leaving moms to claim and cultivate the home turf. By the '50s and '60s, fathering and mothering focused on very separate vocations, in which moms were the "hands-on parents who expressed love and dads were hands-off parents who made money."[12] Most dads were physically and emotionally distant. They were viewed as the breadwinners and "wait until your father gets home" disciplinarians. At home, they often watched television, read the newspaper, and disappeared into a silent, private world. They touched their children only out of necessity, like when helping them dress, and rarely said "I love you," though those are the words every child longs to hear. Then in the '70s, '80s, and '90s, the very value of fathering came into question. Was the presence of a father necessary—or would sperm alone do?

Nowadays? Well, times have changed again, and dads are different! They're more physically and emotionally involved again, thanks to growing research that identifies the importance of a father in a child's life. Dads today want to do more than pay the bills, but with this shift comes a new paradigm of expectations about what makes a good dad.

Great Expectations

From the moment the pregnancy test results come out positive, today's dads are expected to be as intimately involved in the development of that child as he was in the conception! It's common to announce to people, "*We're* pregnant!"

Today's expectant dad is wanted at doctor's appointments, so that he can hear the heartbeat of his unborn baby for the first time and witness the wonder of the first ultrasound. He's scheduled to take childbirth classes in preparation for the delivery, to practice breathing exercises with his wife, and, of course, to be prepared to coach her sensitively and strongly, confidently and carefully, through the delivery. The doctor may even encourage him to be the one to cut the umbilical cord, a highly significant and symbolic gesture.

Then, from the moment the child is born, we moms expect dads to be both gentle and strong, tough and tender, a part of the child's every activity. We want them to care as much as we do about cleanliness and nutrition, to willingly get up in the middle of the night, to manage life's details from laundry to investments while stopping to kiss boo-boos, and to interact relationally with a combination of wisdom and affection. When it comes to parenting, we expect them to "get it," but we also want them to switch instinctively from the role of father to husband, encouraging our development as women in our world, while growing themselves individually and spiritually, and *still* bringing home a salary that will finance the lifestyle of our longings (even if we are working outside ourselves). That's a tall order!

It's not just moms who expect all this of fathers today. Dads expect much of themselves too. When we asked dads to define what makes a good dad, they reported an equal degree of idealism and perfectionism. They passionately want to father and father well.

We began this chapter with definitions of a "good dad" from surveying women just like you. Here is still more of the feedback we got:

A good dad is:

- A man who loves his children, spends time with them, shares common interests, and provides emotional as well as financial support.
- One who disciplines when necessary, but will also laugh and play.
- One who loves his wife.
- One who knows and loves God.

While struggling with the seeming impossibility of meeting both our high standards and their own, dads admit to a certain degree of confusion about what it means to be a good dad these days. No wonder men surveyed by the National Center for Fathering admitted, "Being a father is overwhelming."[13] No wonder one man at a fathering seminar, when asked how he felt about fathering, wrote, "I feel like a dachshund dog running in deep snow."[14] No wonder a father in our survey wrote that "Men are men. . . . We have many things on our minds and we forget so easily. It is really hard to balance everything today with so much going on."

Some fathers let their work become a shield behind which they hide to mask their fears about being good enough fathers. This is called "nest-feathering" by one expert whose research shows that fathers often feel the best way to be a good parent is to be a good "breadwinner" and to "feather the nest" by earning a greater income or career status. The negative side to this approach is the temptation to "run away to work." As one executive put it, "I know how to run a team and make a business plan, but diaper a baby or talk to my son about his feelings? His mother's so good at it, I feel like an oaf."[15]

Because the expectations of fathers have changed so much in the last two generations, many dads today are pioneers in their families when it comes to fathering. The evolving changes mean that many dads today want to father differently than their fathers did. In our survey of fathers, a full 70 percent claim they have different parenting styles than their dads. Consider the interaction between your husband and his father when he became a new dad. Were there honest and tender discussions about the importance of fathering or the feelings of being a new father? Chances are, there were not. Dads today are expected to be more openly loving and caring than their own fathers were.

High Expectations at Home and Work

Dads are dazed not only by the high expectations of what it means to be a good dad at home today, they also face conflicts about how to meet the needs of their children while carrying out their responsibilities at work. Mothers used to be the ones stressed out over the tug of war between home and work responsibilities, but now dads are expressing the same struggles with balance.

When asked what went through his mind when he found out he was going to be a father, one dad, now the father of two, writes, "I had thoughts of the old cliché *Father Knows Best*. I wanted to go out to work and be able to come home with peace and serenity in my heart and enjoy being with my family. But I've discovered there are many outside sources that work against this."[16] James Levine, a "Daddy Stress" seminar leader for companies like Microsoft, Merrill Lynch, and Texas Instruments, comments, "The clash between expectations and responsibilities is a recipe for stress which can boil up into guilt, depression, shoddy work and . . . divorce."[17]

Answers don't come easily, but struggles with priorities and complaints about "not having enough time" are common. In our survey of fathers, the majority of them said that "having more time" would help them be better dads, along with better fatherhood modeling. In another survey, 70 percent of dads say they would take a pay cut to spend more time with their families.[18] But the cost paid is not only in salary! In her book, *Father Courage: What Happens When Men Put Families First,* Suzanne Levine writes, "Women can count on respect if not support, for their choices; men cannot. For a man, it's still professionally risky to behave in any way that suggests that work is not the top priority."[19] In a magazine article entitled "Daddy Stress," the story is told of one CEO who makes evening story time with his three preschoolers a priority, and has to literally shake his employees off his pant leg as he gets into the car in order to follow through on his priority.[20]

SEE "WHAT TO DO NEXT": BABIES AND BUDGETS, PAGE 183.

Dads seem to be getting caught in a "Super-Dad trap" of unrealistic expectations, much like the one moms first experienced in the 1980s. Though many moms still aim for "Super-Mom" performances, others are beginning to feel the freedom to find our way out of the daze of such impossible agendas. Doing it all, doing it all *right* and doing it all *right now* isn't realistic—or necessary. Rather, we are recognizing that our heart desires can stretch out into the many seasons of our lives. With a long hard look at our own unrealistic expectations of ourselves, a healthy dose of creativity, flexibility, sacrifice, and a stubborn commitment, we're slowly making mothering work. It's time for the dads of our day to find their way too, and we can help them by adjusting both our and their expectations. This kind of realistic perspective will free them to be the kind of dads their children need, and to embrace a role they will enjoy!

Make Room for Reflection

- Analyze your expectations for your husband as a father. Are you going for the ideal or the real?

- Sift through the layers of your own heart for what causes you to want so much in a father for your children. Does it touch any needs that you might have?

- Weigh the weight of the world's requirements on you as a mom, and consider how you've come to balance this pressure with the reality of what you can deliver in real time.

- Consider your father's role and your husband's father's role as a parent. How different are your expectations of your husband as a father?

- Review what makes a good dad good by taking the perspective that the father of your children is in process, searching for his own way through the maze of models of fathering, ranging from noninvolvement to total involvement.

Top Tips about Pops from MOPS

- I don't point out differences in the way we do things. . . . That's why children need two role models, so they can adapt and enjoy differences.
- Almost nightly I encourage his playing games with the kids before bed while I clean up from dinner.
- During the times when our children are sick (with throw up in their hair, or appearing shockingly scary because they are so

grossly covered with chicken pox), they need to know that he can still love them.

- I encouraged my husband to take a job on the other end of the county for less money because he would be available more and home more when our child would be awake.
- When he fears he has made the wrong choice for the kids, I try to provide encouragement.

part two **Mommy Style**

chapter three

A Mom's Job:
In the Beginning and Beyond

*H*ey, mom, did you know that good fathering begins with you and your good mothering? Let's think about the meaning of that question.

In the Beginning: Mother Bond

The most amazing bonding begins when a woman discovers she is pregnant. She realizes that she houses the life of another within her own body. She *is* life and breath and sustenance for her unborn child. In fact, the mother's significance in the life of her child—starting with pregnancy—is much more obvious than the vital role the father plays in the life of her child. In order to understand and appreciate your husband's role, then, let's go back to your role as the mother.

When is a mother born? "I think I was born a mother with the first echoes of my baby's heartbeat, which I heard just a few weeks ago. Though not yet in my arms, my infant's heart calls to me, bringing out in me the need to love and protect, to cherish and encourage. With each kick and roll, tuck and twirl, the life dancing inside me confirms what I have just discovered—a mother is born the moment she feels the love in her heart for a child she has never seen."[1]

As we've stated, the mother's bonding process with the baby begins during pregnancy. But when does the baby's awareness of the bonding process with the mother begin? We may not know the exact moment, but let's start from the time a baby emerges from the birth canal and is placed on its mother's tummy, or from the experience of being offered into an adoptive mother's arms.

First, the baby's bond with the mother is *primary.* It is the first bond or attachment forged in the life of an infant. British psychiatrist John Bowlby believed that a baby is programmed to fall in love with his or her mother from birth. A baby is wired to establish an intimate emotional connection with the mother that will influence all later intimate connections, as well as his or her mental stability.[2]

Here's proof of this amazing bond.

- Newborn babies prefer a higher-pitched voice. Not only are most mothers' voices naturally higher than that of a father, but mothers instinctively talk to a newborn in "mother-ese," a voice pitched higher than their usual voices.
- A newborn baby moves in rhythm to his mother's voice, enticing his mother to talk to him more.
- Infants recognize, attend to, and are comforted by their mothers' voices within the first week. Mothers report being able to distinguish their babies' cries from those of other babies while still in the hospital.
- Babies prefer being rocked head to toe—as in a mother's arms—rather than the back-and-forth rocking of a baby swing.
- By the time a baby is five days old, he recognizes and prefers the smell of his own mother's milk.
- A mother's milk provides specific immunities for her child against the germs in their particular environment.[3]

The mother bond is also a *foundational* bond. The mother bond affects the development of her child in various spheres. A baby's brain is a jumble of trillions of neurons, a work in progress, waiting to be wired into a mind. *Newsweek* magazine reported the experiences of early childhood, specifically the basic bond of mother and child, help form the brain's circuits for music, math, language, and emotions. All learning and feelings are built upon the foundation of this bond.[4] Christian psychologists Drs. Henry Cloud and John Townsend report that the hardwiring of an infant's brain— thinking, relating to the world, perceiving, judging, etc.— depends on this bond. In fact, a child's "emotional IQ" is related to his bond with his mother, meaning how to handle failure, troublesome emotions, expectations and ideals, grief and loss. Severe disruption of this attachment in the early months after birth can affect a child's entire life.[5]

And last, the mother bond is *influential* for all other bonds in the child's life. In 1940, Sigmund Freud wrote that a baby's relationship with her mother is "unique, without parallel, established unalterably for a whole lifetime as the first and strongest love object and as the prototype of all later love relationships for both sexes."[6] Attachment expert John Bowlby believed babies need a "secure base" from which to venture out to explore their world. From this base in a kind of hierarchy of attachment figures, a baby develops a sense of his own worthiness, conscience, and the capacity for intimacy in later significant relationships.[7]

No wonder a child's mother is the most important person in her child's early development! And because the mother bond is the central ingredient for all other bonds, your influence is significant for your child's future as well.

Beyond: The Mother's Role in the Father Bond

It feels good to be so needed, doesn't it? Scary and overwhelming at times, yes, but exhilarating to embrace the unique offering of attachment bonding that only a mom can provide in the life of her child.

In fact, attachment through bonding is vital not only for babies but for the healthy development of every human being. As Drs. Cloud and Townsend emphasize, "All of the tasks of life are based, at some level, on how attached we are to God and others. Kids who are emotionally connected in healthy ways are more secure. They delay gratification. They respond to discipline. They deal with failure. They make good moral decisions. The list goes on and on."[8] Doesn't every mother want all this for her child?

SEE "WHAT TO DO NEXT": BECOMING A CHRISTIAN, PAGE 191.

But something subtle can begin to happen in those first few months and years as the powerful bond between mother and child develops. It feels so good to be needed that we sometimes get all tangled up in the attachment and forget the greater purpose of the child's next developmental need. You see, we attach with our infants in order to let them go. That's the goal of the mother bond.

Judith Viorst describes this confusing challenge in her book *Imperfect Control* when she writes about being the "One and Only Indispensable Mommy. The mommy who put on the Band-Aids. The mommy who buttered the bread. The mommy in 'I want Mommy' and 'Mommy's home.' . . . And while all of that need and dependence was often encroaching and sometimes oppressive, there were, in exchange, some exceedingly sweet payoffs. As a friend of mine once observed, 'My son was the only one in my life who squealed with delight whenever I entered a room.'"[9]

While we may like being needed, we need to recognize that this dependence through attachment is what gives a child the confidence to become independent. And the steps toward that healthy independence start with separation from the mother, which is part of the child's next developmental need.

Get it? Attachment—the mother bond—can achieve its intended purpose in a child's development only if we use it as a foundation for launching: allowing and encouraging the child to establish other bonds with dad, friends, a future mate, and God.

Yes, the mother holds the primary bond. She is the apex of the baby's relational pyramid; the touchstone for his growth as he goes out to others and returns to her for security checks.[10] And she is the major influence on all other attachments. But she is not sufficient in herself to meet all of the child's needs. Her job is to teach her infant to attach securely and safely to her so that he can attach with others as he grows. The attachment to mom is where the child learns and practices for relationships elsewhere.

With an understanding of this foundation, we can then say that the most important action in a mother's job *after* attaching is launching. The mother bond influences the success of the first *other* bond: the father bond.

The importance of this first step in letting go is critical. In fact, Drs. Henry Cloud and John Townsend claim that one of the greatest problems in American culture today is the difficulties that many moms have in creating room for the father to take his place in the life of the child. That's because mothers often don't understand this hinge point in the child's development, nor do they understand how to encourage the child's bonding to the father.

This problem may also grow out of a mom's personal issues that subtly affect her mothering. She might get her own needs mixed up with her child's needs. She might need to be needed, or seek to fix her own loneliness or emptiness with her child. Maybe she didn't grow up with good modeling when it comes to parenting, or she doesn't have a good relationship with the father of her child. We'll look at some of these common issues in later chapters, but for now let's focus on the establishment of the father bond.

SEE "WHAT TO DO NEXT": WISDOM FOR MOMS, PAGE 186.

In the first few weeks of a baby's life, a father is highly involved in giving the child the best mom possible. He frees mom to be the baby's secure and consistent lifeline by taking over many of life's other details. He might run errands, load and unload the dishwasher, or do the laundry. Meanwhile, mom is meeting an infant's most vital needs. But slowly, the baby needs to expand his world. As he or she gains a sense of safety and secure attachment, the baby then expresses a need for autonomy or separation, called *individuation* by child experts. This is a baby's perfectly normal developmental need to see himself or herself as separate from mom, and happens at about six to eight months. It is at this time that the baby naturally begins to move toward daddy, the first other bond in the child's life.

Mom's role is to allow and encourage the attachment to dad by creating the space for dad to care for the child, even when some of the ways he will nurture the baby will be different from her own. She can let him make "his way" with the baby without interfering too quickly or taking responsibility for the way dad interacts with the baby.[11]

James Barron describes a typical conversation between mom and dad when dad is taking care of the baby:

She (nervous): "What do you think you're doing?"

He (Frank Sinatra tone): "I'm doing it my way!"

She (anxious): "Well, your way is too slow."

He (defensively): "My way seems all right for me and the baby."

She (livid): "Never mind. Just hand her to me. I'll do it myself."[12]

This father advises other new fathers to "just do it your way" in these day-to-day interactions. Tucked into these words is a message for moms: let dad do it his way.

Both Mother and Father Bonds

Both parents provide their children with a secure base from which to go out and explore their world. While the mother bond may be significant because it is the first bond, the father bond is equally vital because it is the first other bond.

While both are important bonds, they are formed differently. The mother attaches to her child mainly through caretaking; the father bonds through play.[13] It's been said that by the time a baby is three to four weeks old, an observer can look at the baby's face, not knowing with whom she is playing, and successfully tell who is interacting with the baby: mother, father, or stranger. With a mother, the baby's movements and facial expressions are smooth and rhythmic, anticipating a calm, low-key interaction. With a father, the baby tenses up, her face lights up, and movements become agitated, in anticipation of father play.[14]

Once again, attachment to both parents is necessary for healthy bonding to others. As Drs. Cloud and Townsend summarize, "The child must experience the reality that relationship is good and that it brings the necessary elements of life. When your child learns this emotionally, he structures his existence to seek relationship to sustain him. He becomes relationally-oriented rather than self-oriented."[15] Now, that's healthy. And what more could you want than a healthy kid!

SEE "WHAT TO DO NEXT": THE ABCS OF LOVE, PAGE 177.

How are you doing, mom? Feeling empowered? We hope so. We've discussed that the mother bond is primary, foundational, and influential. A mother's job in this mother bond is to prepare her child for the first other bond: the father bond. One writer describes a mom's job as becoming a "promoting mother," one who brings her husband into the spotlight rather than keeping him in the wings, one who brings him into the experience of parenthood frequently and openly by sharing everything from the physical sensations of pregnancy to the first diaper change.[16]

In other words, mom, you have the greatest influence on your husband's success as a dad. You can either help or hurt his effectiveness in the life of his child. When you recognize and encourage the unique offerings that he brings to his child, you are helping him be the kind of dad your child needs— and the kind of dad God created him to be!

Make Room for Reflection

- Look back over how you bonded with your baby. What was the process like? Where was it difficult?

- Consider some of the ways you bonded with your baby. How can you re-create some of those experiences for dad and his child? Maybe begin by reflecting on how you feel about the baby bonding with another person. What emotions does it arouse in you? Tenderness? Amazement? Is there any insecurity or jealousy? Why might this be?

- In what ways has your baby changed since beginning to bond with his or her dad?

Top Tips about Pops from MOPS

- I try to set my husband up for success by letting the kids over-hear me bragging about them to him. Then he goes and asks them about what they did that was good. They really connect with him at those times, celebrating little triumphs together.
- I give him opportunities to take our oldest daughter out on special dates—just the two of them.
- I always talk to the girls positively about daddy: "He's the best daddy in the world, isn't he?"
- I get to hear the "fresh from school" tales, and they're not so eager to retell the stories five hours later when dad gets home. So I assist the conversation a bit by offering questions for him to ask or by reminding the kids of things they could tell their dad.
- When he's around, I let my husband take care of bumps and bruises. That way the kids don't think that mom is the only one who can make them feel better.
- When we're in church and one of the boys wants me to hold him, I may say, "Maybe Daddy will hold you." Even though I really want to hold him, it gives him special time with his daddy.

chapter four

Heart Longings

*D*oes anything in the following story remind you of yourself?

Terri woke up to the sound of the baby crying. She rolled over and looked at the clock. 5:53 A.M. Why did she feel so tired? She'd gone to bed about nine o'clock last night, shortly after getting the baby and three-year-old Lisa tucked in. And her husband, Bob, had gotten up to feed the baby at 2 A.M. just as he'd promised—after she nudged him awake. She couldn't understand why the baby's cries didn't wake him. Why didn't he respond like she did? Probably his snoring drowned out the crying. Like now. Terri crawled quietly out of bed, pulled on her robe, and headed down the hall to feed the baby. Her day had begun.

Nearly an hour later, Bob wandered into the kitchen, poured himself a cup of coffee, and tried to kiss Terri's cheek as she balanced the baby on one hip and poured cereal for Lisa with her free hand. She turned away from his kiss, so he planted the errant smooch on the baby's forehead. "Hey, you and me had a good time dancing together around the living room in the middle of the night, didn't we?" he smiled at the baby, who gave him a toothless grin in response.

"Honey, did you feed her while you were dancing? I think that upsets her tummy. She seems a little cranky this morning. And did you put too much of that stuff on her diaper rash?" Terri asked. "It looks all gunky." Even as she spoke, she knew the word *honey* didn't mask the edge of her irritation.

Bob paused, coffee cup in midair. The grin disappeared from his face. "Terri, you know," he spoke slowly, searching her face, "I'm not as good a mom as you are, but I try. And I guess I just didn't do it right. Again. Maybe I just can't please you." With that, he turned and walked out of the kitchen.

"Mommy, what's wrong with Daddy?" Lisa asked.

"I don't know, honey," Terri answered. But silently she wondered. *Maybe nothing is wrong with him. Maybe this is about me, not him. Why do I pick at him like that? What is wrong with me?*

We hear these questions from moms over and over. "Why do I do what I do? What is this nagging feeling that sometimes gnaws away at my heart and makes me yearn for something I don't have? What is wrong with me, and why do I treat my husband that way?"

These questions grow out of the longings of our hearts, those hard-to-describe yearnings for something we don't have but think we want. We watch chick flicks and read romance novels and buy self-help books that promise a better body, better sex life, better relationships. We seek perfect friends, perfect husbands, perfect dads, perfect children, even perfect fingernails. And of course, something or someone always falls a bit short and we're left, mystified, to deal with the leftover longings still gnawing away at our hearts.

What's this all about?

It's about being women and being normal and being created with a heart longing to be loved well—and to know that we are loving others well. This heart longing is a good longing. It is foundational to our desire to be good wives and good moms and to give our children the best, including a good dad. But this heart longing can also cause us to hold ourselves back from the good we could do in helping our husbands be good fathers.

A Woman's Heart

The cause of our longings is rooted in our hearts as women. We were made for relationships. The very first woman was named Eve, the mother of all living. Further, Eve was created in order to be a companion to the living man, Adam. No, we don't have to conceive and give birth to life in order to be fulfilled in life. We don't have to be in a marriage relationship in order to be fulfilled. But in a sense, we do indeed need to be *in relationship* in order to be fulfilled in life.

Our need for relationship becomes clear when we consider the girlfriend front. We know what it's like to need a soul mate, a mom, or another woman who's "been there and done that" in the stages of motherhood. Yes, indeed—how would we ever have made it this far without such everyday wisdom!

The bigger reason for such focus on relationship is that we women are created in the image of a God who longs for relationship himself. As Sharon Hersh explains in her book *Brave Hearts,* "Our longings for relationships are relentless reminders of what we were made for and what is worth living for. . . . Not only is our longing for relationships an integral part of us, but it is a reflection of the heart of God."[1]

Psychologist John Townsend underlines our need for relationship with the term *belonging.* Our sense of longing is answered with an experience of belonging. He writes, "At the deepest spiritual and emotional level, we are emotional beings who need safety and a sense of belonging in our three primary relationships: God, self, and others. We begin life in a terrified and disconnected state. . . . It is the deepest and most fundamental problem we can experience."[2] As we move through life, fulfillment becomes possible as we engage over and over again in meaningful relationships whose purposes are clear and whose goals are met.

SEE "WHAT TO DO NEXT": SUPPORT GROUPS FOR YOU, PAGE 163.

Although women were made for relationships, we're not always healthy in the ones we inhabit. Several factors influence these heart longings in our role as mom.

Your Father's Influence

Your father may have filled you with so many demonstrations of his love that it is next to impossible to find such a satisfying example in your days, and you unknowingly reject all lesser approaches. With such a model in your past, your expectations reach mammoth proportions for your dear husband as the father of your children. "My father was a great dad," one mother wrote. "He spent one-on-one time with me every day. He is the one who would tuck me in bed. He gave me lots of hugs and kisses and always told me he loved me. . . . As a little girl, my one goal in life was to marry my dad." You long for a repeat performance of your father's success in the lives of your children and yet find yourself uneasy with your husband's efforts. How can he ever fill your father's shoes?

On the other hand, your father may have disappointed you so deeply, so intensely, so completely, so devastatingly, that you possess no template of the inherent potential in the father-child relationship for your children. Fathers seem dispensable, unnecessary to your self-sufficient, survivor style. It's easier to take over and do fathering functions rather than risk a repeat rejection of yourself in the lives of your little ones. Beneath such a scar lies a tender wound yet to be healed.

Your Husband's Influence

Your own husband also influences these heart longings for relationship as he fathers your children. If he isn't like your dad, you may wish for him to be different. "My father was a very hands-on father in all the day-to-day childrearing activities," one mother writes. "I wish my children's father would be more hands-on with everyday activities just out of a desire to be involved, not because he feels it is his obligation to do so." Another writes, "I wish my husband would do more of the physical things for our son, such as bathing, dressing, and changing diapers. I remember my father helping my mom with everything."

If he is awkward in his approach to parenting, holding back in moments of insecurity, you may conclude that your husband doesn't have what it takes, and rush in to remedy by taking over the care of the children entirely on your own. If he's made a few overtures and then given up, you may give up as well, resigning yourself to a hopelessness that he'll never get the hang of it and therefore never provide for your child's—and your—needs for a father in the family.

These and other heart longings confuse our hearts and leave us more than muddled as moms when we face a major challenge of mothering: launching our child from the mother bond to the first other bond: the father bond.

SEE "WHAT TO DO NEXT": HIDDEN STUFF IN YOUR HEART, PAGE 155.

A Confused Heart

Unsatisfied heart longings for relationships can lead us down two wrong paths of thinking. First, we can confuse our needs with the needs of our child. Because you need to feel valuable and needed, you might conclude that your child primarily needs you and is not ready for another bond. Because your baby seems happiest when you change and bathe him, you might decide that he prefers you to anyone else. Because you enjoy the upwardly stretched arms of your toddler's greeting, you may determine that this is a "mommy" signal and rush to scoop him up in your arms before anyone else has a chance to respond.

Second, as mothers we can become confused about what makes us significant. This is another kind of need for affirmation. We feel so good to be so needed by our little one that we begin to find our significance in our ability to meet our child's needs. And why not? All that incredible stuff about the mother bond being primary, foundational, and influential—it's unbelievably validating! The concept of stepping back, sharing the significance with another, launching *my baby* to the lap of another, can feel threatening, like you might lose something precious. Many new moms are actually terrified that daddy might be as good as they are at this business of taking care of baby. Then what? As Vicki Iovine puts it, "Many of us already secretly suspect that we are really amateurish at this mothering business, and if a *man*, someone whom God did not see fit to bless with a uterus, can do the job proficiently, then our self-esteem and identity lie in shattered little pieces on the nursery floor."[3]

Then third, there's the fear that the child might start loving daddy best. One mom describes this fear: "At our house every day around five o'clock, my oldest child erupts into joyous calls of 'Daddy's home, Daddy's home!' Of course we are all happy to see him, but I used to be a little jealous. Andrew always tugged at my husband from the minute he got home until bedtime. I felt like he loved Daddy more than me."[4]

When we immerse ourselves in the vital mother bond, we can become confused that we matter *only* when we are the *only ones* who matter. Sharing significance may feel like losing it.

A Free Heart

Freedom comes when we recognize that we were created for relationship and that all relationships have their purpose. The mother-child relationship is free when the mother understands that her bonding is for the child's launching. The mother-father relationship is free when it grasps that two parents function in tandem to meet the needs of the child.

Freedom also comes when a mother recognizes her heart longings, even those that grow out of having an incomplete relationship with her own father, and she moves on to celebrate the differences in her husband. One mom responding to our survey wrote, "I learned through some hard times how important a father figure is in a woman's life. I am thirty-two and still long to have a relationship with my daddy. My husband knows how important it is to start a relationship with his girls at a very young age in order to have one in the teenage and older years of their lives. I melt inside when they want their daddy instead of their mommy because I know then that there is already a special bond started."

Remember the mom quoted earlier in this chapter who feared that her child loved her husband more than he loved her because of his excitement when daddy came home each day? She found freedom in identifying the source of her fear, and recognized her longing for a better relationship with her child. She realized that she had been spending all of her time taking care of business and running her household at the expense of time spent playing with her child. When she rearranged her priorities, she discovered a new joy in her own relationship with her child.

SEE "WHAT TO DO NEXT": PRACTICING FORGIVENESS, PAGE 156.

Foundational to freedom in relationships is the fact that we all find our needs most deeply met when we are in the one sacred relationship designed to meet them fully: a relationship with the God who made us in the first place. We were never meant to be alone in mothering or in life! We were created for relationship with a God who loves us deeply. When we understand who we are in him, there is much freedom to receive and give our own offering, and to leave others to receive and give theirs.

This may be a new concept for you. Or it may be a familiar thought which is now taking on new meaning as you mother. In either case, take time to explore what this means to you.

> SEE "WHAT TO DO NEXT": BECOMING A CHRISTIAN, PAGE 191,
> AND WHAT IS A REAL CHRISTIAN? PAGE 187.

A mother with a free heart distinguishes between mothering and fathering and moves out of dad's way while investing herself wholly in mothering. She understands by learning to let go. She bonds in order to release. She feels secure about who she is and recognizes that she is constantly growing and changing and becoming, even in the midst of her mothering, and that she doesn't need to be "everything" for her child. She knows she is not perfect, but she's good enough because she is in process. In their book *The Mom Factor*, Drs. Henry Cloud and John Townsend describe this kind of honest freedom as the "good-enough" mother. "Good enough moms are aware of their weaknesses and tendencies. They are working on doing the right thing for themselves and their child."[5]

A mother with a free heart seeks wholeness in a variety of relationships, including her mothering. She fills the longings of her heart by mothering as well as she can and, in so doing, makes room for daddy in the life of her child.

Make Room for Reflection

- Listen to your heart longings. They are normal and part of the heart of every woman who is alive and breathing and growing. So try not to mask or ignore them. Try to identify these longings by asking yourself a few questions. What do you desire more than anything else in the world? What dreams do you have for yourself in life? Consider your relationships. How would you like to improve them? Think about some things that could make you happy but have failed to do so. Take out a piece of paper and write some of these thoughts down.

- Think about your father. How does your husband match up? Is he better or not? Think about what you long for in your husband as a father to your children. What qualities does he already possess? Where do you wish he would grow? How can you move out of the way to encourage his bond with his child?

- Let your longings lead you to their Source. God created you with these longings for relationships. How might he want to be in your life to meet them? Do you read the Bible? Have you ever prayed? Who is farther along the journey in knowing God and could serve as a guide for you?

- Remember your goal as a mom: to launch your child into the world. In *The Girlfriends' Guide to Surviving the First Year of Motherhood,* Vicki Iovine gives us a reality check by reminding us that as mothers, "The big goal is to teach your child to get by in the world without you, not to guarantee that all her needs must be met by Mommy."[6]

Top Tips about Pops from MOPS

- I encourage him to get involved with school activities, helping at class parties and reading to our second grader's class during reading week.
- When they go camping, I don't interfere with the packing. If they forget things, it seems to end up okay.
- I told my husband one time that I found it sexy to watch him play with and enjoy our kids. He makes it a point now to play with the kids. I still find it sexy.
- One time I bought cute little prom purses for the girls and gave them to him. He then gave them to the girls and they were thrilled with his gift.

chapter five

Mind Warps

When moms get together and talk about what they want most in life, they quickly discover a common desire. More than anything, moms long to be good moms. That means meeting the needs of their children and giving them the best, which includes giving them a good dad.

This is clear thinking. It makes sense. And good moms can't be faulted for such a good passion. But along the journey to "good mom-dom," we can take a false turn. In wanting to give our child the best, we might conclude that we are responsible for making sure they have a good dad. The key phrase here is "we are responsible." In other words, we think it's all up to us.

Now, moms do play an important role in this result. A foundational principle of this book is that moms have a great deal of influence on what kind of dads their husbands will become. But we also can get distracted and confused about our responsibility for that result. As mentioned in the last chapter, our heart longings can distract us from the good we could do in influencing our husbands' fathering. Heart longings can confuse us and keep us from the vital role we play in launching our child to bond with dad and others. Recognizing and understanding our heart longings as women and mothers helps us fulfill these desires in healthy ways—specifically in a relationship with the one who created us with these longings: God.

As women who are made for relationships, we not only long with our hearts. Sometimes our heads get involved and we actually begin to *believe* certain untruths about our needs and how to have them met. We move from heart longings to "mind warps."

Specific mind warps affect our mothering and influence our husbands' fathering. Common to these warped perspectives is the issue of control. One kind of mind warp—we call it "Mother Superior"—assumes too much control. We think we know it all, and therefore must do it all: both mothering and fathering. Another mind warp—this one is called "Martyr Mom"—relinquishes control *and* personal responsibility. When moms struggle with their value, they may give up their voices as mothers, not to mention their influence on their husbands' fathering.

Let's look at these two specific mind warps, or skewed perspectives, which may be a part of our style of mothering.

Mother Superior

Consider the following scene. Mom and dad are watching TV with baby between them on the couch. Baby starts to fuss. Dad picks up baby, sticks a pacifier in her mouth, and lifts her high above his head, as if to distract her, but baby keeps crying. Mom takes baby from dad's arms saying, "Here, hon, I'll take her. I think I know what she needs." Was dad doing something wrong? Did he not know what baby needed? Did mom really know best? What is the message dad received in that exchange?

Men as well as women assume that moms know more about kids. "I have an intuition about our child that my husband doesn't," wrote a mom in our survey. "I seem to understand her toddler talk." Call it maternal instinct or whatever, but "when a woman does something with a child, it's immediately assumed she's doing it correctly. She can do some truly strange things, and no one calls her on it. Sometimes men feel no matter what a man does with a child, some woman is bound to peer over his shoulder questioning why he's doing it that way."[1]

One mom stated, "I see myself as 100 hundred percent responsible [for the children] and dad is the helper." Society at large agrees. In the health department, even if both parents are present at a child's appointment, most eye contact and questions are addressed toward mom.[2] One dad commented, "I walk in the door and relinquish my opinion. I immediately figure that my wife knows exactly what to do and that whatever she says will be better than whatever I would come up with. I'm beginning to recognize that I don't do this in any other area of my life."

This "mother knows best" stance can be labeled "maternal supremacy." It feels good. It's validating. It's control based on superior knowledge. But is it based in truth?

In our other books about mothering, we've written about the significance of a mother's role and have underlined and encouraged a mom's irreplaceable contribution to the life of her child by saying things like, "No one can mother your child the way you can" or "You are the mother your child needs." And even, "There is an instinctive leading to mother which must be recognized and encouraged." In other chapters in this book, we've written about the vital importance of the mother bond, the primary bond in a child's life, which is necessary before a child can move on to the first other bond (the father bond) and other bonds beyond that.

All these descriptions of mother love and bonds are indeed true. But the fact that no one else can take the place of our offering in the life of our child is no reason to adopt an attitude of superiority that assumes any other offering of love is therefore *less* important than ours. While our children greatly need our investment in their lives, they also need the investment of their father and many others around them.

There is no doubt that moms know a lot. And they also do a lot. Moms usually spend more time caring for a baby in that infant's first few months of life. They get to know their child intimately. But research demonstrates—in a variety of forms—that fathers are also sensitive and responsive to their infants' needs. They know when something is wrong with the baby, and they act to meet those needs too.[3] Further, at a very young age, babies are able to elicit competent, loving caretaking not only from female but also from male adults.[4]

These findings seem to prove that a father has the ability to parent well. So why are we and the world around us so quick to seize upon the concept of maternal supremacy which feeds the image of Mother Superior? Judith Viorst, in her insightful and often humorous look at the role of power in our lives, suggests that mothers may find in their mothering role "the power that has eluded them all of their lives, their self-esteem buoyed by their function as 'the mother who always knows best, who knows what to do and how to do it, who knows what is right, what is good, and what is of value.' Such a mother . . . thrives in her newfound omnipotent-care-taker role."[5]

Surprising though it may seem, research shows that two out of three women actually seem threatened by equal participation and may themselves be unintentionally putting a damper on men's involvement with their children because they are possessive of their role as primary nurturer.[6] Without realizing it, we discourage dads' efforts.

Think of it this way. We want to be good moms. More than anything. We want our children to have the best. We know our child needs a good dad, and he seems to want to be one, but he's a bit unsteady. So at the first sign that he is wavering, feeling confused adjusting to his new role, entangled in the net of expectations, we dive in and take over. We adjust, edit, interpret, teach, correct, and claim the turf because we know what to do and why. We are, after all, Mother Superior.

But we soon learn that such an attempt is exhausting. It doesn't work in the long run, and it's not what our kids need. They don't need us to father them; they need us to mother them—and to make room for daddy.

SEE "WHAT TO DO NEXT": WHEN YOU NEED HELP, PAGE **164.**

Martyr Mom

Instead of taking control, this way of mothering abdicates control to others through silent compliance. The mom who enters into this mind warp finds comfort by acting in a way she thinks she should act, or the way she thinks others think she should act. Her model may have been handed down by her own mother or from a model her husband or someone else handed her. Through silent compliance, a Martyr Mom often masks her real feelings.

Most of us admire Martyr Moms. On the outside of their smiling presentation, they appear serene, at ease, calm. Their ordered lives run smoothly. While there's nothing wrong with such outer peace, concern comes when the woman within is disconnected from herself. The Martyr Mom doesn't really know who she is or what she wants. Trapped in a life based on fulfilling everyone else's expectations for her and definitions of her value, her heart shrinks.

The Martyr Mom is a mom who has lost her sense of self— and her voice. In an effort to produce security for herself and therefore for her children, she ignores her own needs. She dismisses her own ideas. She mistrusts her instincts. She questions her viewpoints. Instead, she "hands over" control—and pieces of personal responsibility—to others. She does and feels what is expected of her, hushing her internal uncertainties.

In silencing her own mothering voice, the Martyr Mom surrenders her opportunity to influence her husband's fathering and his offering to his children.

SEE "WHAT TO DO NEXT": GRUMPY OR GRATEFUL: IT'S UP TO YOU, PAGE 152.

Mind warps are skewed perspectives or wrong beliefs—usually based on the unmet or unrealized longings of our hearts—that impact our husbands' fathering. How are you doing, mom? The journey from heart longing to mind warp is subtle, and the identification of Mother Superior or Martyr Mom traits are often surprising when we recognize them in ourselves. Take heart. There is much hope. The choice to change is a real choice. And it belongs to each of us as moms.

Make Room for Reflection

- Examine the concept of being a Mother Superior in your own life. Are there ways in which you think you know better or best when it comes to mothering? Which aspects hold some truth in that you *do* in fact know better? Why do you know better in those areas? Now, where might you and your husband be equally new at a piece of parenting?

- How can you encourage your husband to discover and gain confidence in his own knowledge as a parent?

- In marriage, we are so tempted to try to change each other. There's an old saying that "opposites attract ... until they get married." Those "opposite" traits that we liked in our dating days become the very things we try to change in our spouses once we are married. We fall into this pattern so subtly that we often don't recognize what we are doing. Ken Canfield and Nancy Swihart write, "It's as much for *your* own sake that you should not try to change your husband. It will introduce a dynamic that will poison your relationship and undermine your best intentions. Instead of trying to change him, simply do what you believe God has called you to do in relation to him and his fathering. Your faithfulness is within your control—the results are not."[7] In what ways are you trying to change your husband? Name one way you will intentionally change that pattern.

• Which mind warp—Mother Superior or Martyr Mom—most closely describes you? Give an example of where you see it evidenced in your mothering. What can you do to shift away from this mind warp?

Tops Tips about Pops from MOPS

• I enrolled my oldest (age four) and her father in a parent-child sports class.
• I frequently encourage my husband to talk on the phone to the kids when he is out of town, even to our two-year-olds, who don't really talk yet.
• I work part-time on Saturdays and have to let go and let him handle things without worrying about how they are done.
• I usually remind him to make sure that he keeps his promises.

chapter six

A Mom's Choice:
Puppet or Partner?

I would like to be a little bigger. Look at me! I've never been more than a Tom Thumb."

"But you can't grow," answered the fairy.

"Why not?"

"Because puppets never grow. They are born puppets, they live puppets and they die puppets."

"I'm sick of being a puppet!" cried Pinocchio, slapping his wooden head. "It's about time I became a real man, like other people!"

—Carlo Collodi, *The Adventures of Pinocchio*

As moms, we have a choice in how we influence our husbands' fathering. Will we take hold of the "strings" of his fathering and set about to control and manipulate the style of his investment in his children? Or will we step back and allow him to be the "real" and unique dad he longs to be?

Puppeteering

How tempting it is to put dads in the puppet role. How easy! "Sure, he's the head of the household," one mom said, "but I'm the neck that turns the head."

Dads are often viewed this way. "Dad" in name only, but distanced in their fathering. Not as involved as mom, physically or emotionally. Not as capable. As one author puts it,

73

"Large numbers [of fathers] are emotionally remote and function as appendages to mothers in the basic care of their children."[1] As we stated in the last chapter, some moms see themselves as totally in charge and dads as the helpers called in by moms to assist in the task of parenting. This "calling the shots" by mom puts her in control. Society at large reinforces such a stance by often stereotyping a man as less equipped than a woman to parent.

Consider the following example: A mom exits the jetway of an airplane, baby and carry-on bag in her arms. She looks determined, directed, and focused on the goal of getting to the next gate for a connecting flight. There is a lull before the next individual emerges from the plane. Before he becomes visible, the mom turns around. "Honey, pick Benjamin up. He can't walk fast enough," she orders, and then adds, "Oh, be careful! Everything's falling out of the bag!"

Soon a man exits the jetway, trying to zip up the diaper bag hanging from his shoulder while also juggling an infant seat, folded-up stroller, and a squirming, whiny two-year-old. "Here, I'll take the bag," the mom continues as the family heads down the concourse. "You are jiggling Benjy too much. He's tired and upset. Just be gentle with him. And wipe his nose. Yuk! But not like that. More gently!" Her corrections continue as they head toward the gate.

It's as if she picks up her husband's invisible strings and adjusts first one puppet leg and then the other, manipulating him toward their destination. Sure, she is also laden with baby and bags, but she still believes she can manage his movement better than he can manage it himself. A Mother Superior mom is someone like this.

The problem with puppeteering is a problem with boundaries. Drs. Henry Cloud and John Townsend define a boundary as "what is me and what is not me. A boundary shows me where I end and someone else begins, lending a sense of own-ership."[2] We face a struggle with boundaries when we get our responsibilities mixed up with our husbands' responsibilities. We become confused regarding what we should own and what we should not own.

The puppet picture, and the question about boundaries, can happen just as easily with the roles reversed.

Let's go back to the airport. This time, the dad emerges first. Diaper bag slung over his shoulder, he pauses to take the tickets out of the pocket of his jacket. He checks the mon-itor for the next gate, then looks back over his shoulder for his wife. She finally exits the jetway, pushing baby in the stroller with the toddler's help, while also balancing her carry-on case. She searches the crowd, finds her husband, and looks depend-ently toward him, unsure of where to turn and what to do next. The baby cries and she pulls the toddler close to her, taking her eyes off her husband just as he sets off down the concourse. Once she finally settles her infant and looks up, her husband is nowhere in sight. When she realizes she has no tickets and no knowledge of the flight number or next gate, she feels helpless. So she gathers her toddler, turns the stroller toward a row of seats, and plunks down to wait. Surely, he'll return when he realizes they aren't with him.

Now who's the puppet? Without realizing it, this mom has placed the "strings" of her life in her husband's hands and hangs under his control. To mask her sense of helplessness and fill the emptiness caused by her loss of self, she turns all her attention toward her children, like a Martyr Mom, who has ceased thinking about her own needs.

Puppeteering can go either way in a marriage. In an effort to make parenting work "better," either mom or dad can pick up the strings of the other's life and begin to manipulate toward a goal, or lay down his or her own responsibilities under the control of the spouse. In the first example in the airport, the mother may have developed the habit of mothering on her own. Watching her husband do things his way is too uncomfortable, so she takes over. As one mother in our survey said, "I am the one who wears the pants in the family. . . . I am the leader who wants it to go my way, and he wants things to be peaceful and is more likely to give in."

In the second example, the mother lets her husband have total control. But both ways are skewed. Our responsibility as adults is to be clear about what we can and can't control, who we are and who we are not. As Drs. Cloud and Townsend tell us in *Boundaries,* we are not responsible *for* other people. We are responsible *to* others and *for* ourselves.[3] We cannot control or change others, nor should we try. When we do, our efforts are seen as manipulative by the other person, as described here by Ken Canfield, founder of the National Center for Fathering: "If we men perceive that our wives are trying to change us, then we'll view even their best intentions as manipulative scheming. Forgive our pigheadedness, but it's really human nature."[4] We can control and change only ourselves.

So if we want to influence and encourage our husbands' fathering in a positive manner, we should move away from the puppet role of control and move toward that of partner instead.

Partnering

We've said it already. Children need both their moms and dads. They need dad to be the way he is. Moms need dads to be dads too. We were made to be in relationship as we parent. Sure, not all of us can be, but most have that option either as a married couple, or as a divorced or unmarried mom who chooses to work together with her child's father in the task of parenting.

The answer to parenting is not puppeteering; it's partnering. When a child comes into a marriage, everything changes, including your relationship, your perspective, and your priorities. You and your husband will grow and stretch in many new directions, and the challenge is to grow and stretch together. Learning to weather these changes as partners is part of a process that is perfected over time. Several insights strengthen this partnership in the midst of parenting.

Take Up Teamwork

Like oxen yoked together pulling a load in the same direction, parents who are partners strengthen and support each other as they move toward the goal of raising healthy kids. If one stumbles or gets sick, the other has to pull harder, but one can't pull the whole load alone; it's too much. You get much farther if you are both pulling.

Ruth Barton describes how such teamwork has boosted her mothering and her husband's fathering. "The most encouraging thing that has happened for me as a mother is that Chris (my husband) and I have begun seeing ourselves more clearly as a team in this challenge-of-a-lifetime called parenting. I have found that I do not need another book on how to be a better mother. . . . What I have needed is my husband, the father of these children, to participate more fully with me in this great call of God upon our lives. I have needed to hear him say with words and with action, 'You are not alone. These children are just as much my responsibility as they are yours.'"[5]

Obvious venues for teamwork include caring for children. Be careful to omit the word *baby-sitting* from your vocabulary when you or your husband is on duty with your children. Neither one of you is baby-sitting when you are on solo duty; you are parenting. Baby-sitting implies a temporary taking over of responsibilities, whereas parenting denotes shared responsibilities.

Other opportunities for teamwork include the delegation of household chores. While some tasks are viewed culturally as belonging to the male or the female, few must actually be handled on a gender basis. Make a list of all that has to be done and how much time is available and then delegate according to interest, skill, and experience. Trade off doing really yucky chores.

SEE "WHAT TO DO NEXT": BATTLE OF THE CHORES: WHO DOES WHAT? PAGE **160.**

A word of caution: remember the lessons of early marriage when it was easy to cling to a chore because "your mother did it that way" or you didn't think he'd do it the "right way" (your way). Most likely, you ended up doing most of the tasks yourself. Unless you've caught and corrected this pattern, it's likely to have followed you all the way through to patterns of parenting. A *Wall Street Journal* article titled "Women Pay a Price for Control" states, "The reality is that many women, even those who have full-time jobs, still take great pride in their ability to run and manage the home. Giving up responsibilities at home means giving up a piece of your identity and losing a daily source of affirmation. And it means giving up an important source of power and control."[6]

Beware of other subtle areas where you might be taking over control in parenting without being aware of it. *Gatekeeping* is the term sociologists use in describing how the powerful love of the mother can sometimes close the emotional gate between a father and child. In his book *Real Boys,* William Pollack, Ph.D., writes, "As close as mother and father may become through mutual parenting, sometimes they can fall into patterns that draw them apart, and actually make it tougher to feel good about themselves as parents." He goes on to explain that some fathers may find it hard to stay closely involved in nurturing their sons if their wives engage in unconscious gatekeeping. That happens when mothers, despite their very best intentions, unwittingly maintain so close a bond with their sons that there is simply little room left for the father to play a meaningful role. An example would be to correct dad when he's holding or rocking the baby. "Don't hold him like that" or "Don't rock him that way." The dad, who already feels inadequate, usually gives his son back to mom and backs off. His imagined or real deficiencies lead him to shy away from other opportunities to connect with his son.[7] In this way, the process of teamwork is thwarted.

Define Your Mission

Define together the big-picture purpose of your family and your parenting. This is your "mission statement," and it might not be clear at first. Set aside some time to talk about your own values and which ones you want to impart to your children. What are your goals in parenting? What qualities do you admire in other families? What do you each think regarding subjects like finances, work, traditions, extended family, and faith? Take a stab at shaping these into a mission statement, such as: "What matters most to our family is love: loving God and each other." Or, "We want to be an inward and outward family. We will love each other well so that we can love others well." Then give some more time to intentionally applying the values and goals in your statement to your day-to-day challenges. Let your ideas grow and change as you grow and change together. Keep talking about your goals. Family missions are refocused often due to the changes in a family over seasons of development.

SEE "WHAT TO DO NEXT": BABIES AND BUDGETS, PAGE 183.

Communicate Clearly

Good communication includes listening, talking, and resolving. First, listen for what your husband is saying, not just for what you want to hear or what you want to say back once he's finished. What are the feelings behind his words? If you listen to understand, you're actually putting aside *your* agenda and pricking up your ears to hear *his*.

Second, talk. Your husband can't read your mind or your thoughts. You need to put your feelings and thought into words, as hard as that may seem. Some communication experts recommend using word pictures to get your point across more clearly. Try using an analogy or example that helps your husband relate to what you're saying about your feelings: "As a mom, I'm like the quarterback and we're late in the fourth quarter of a tied game on third down with long yardage. I feel like the pressure is totally on me to turn things around and make something happen!"

Third, resolve. Conflict is an inevitable part of marriage. Instead of avoiding it, denying it, or flying in its face with aggressive defenses, expect it. Even plan for it. Resolution usually involves compromise—rarely is either person all wrong or all right. But if you see those times of conflict as opportunities to learn to work through something together, you will strengthen your partnership.

Learning to use good communication skills will bring dividends even beyond your marriage relationship. When you learn to communicate with love and truth, you will find that you also strengthen your communication with your children and vice versa. What you invest in one relationship ripples out and reaps rewards in all other family relationships.

Tend to Your Marriage

If you are married to the father of your children, this is one of those "duh" statements: You have to tend to your marriage in the midst of parenting.

In her book *Marriage 911,* Becky Freeman writes, "Baby arrives. Man watches lover turn into mother. Man misses wife. Woman feels pulled in two. Baby drains energy needed for couple to do anything about it. Just when life gets under control, the home pregnancy test turns blue again."[8]

In our book *Children Change a Marriage,* we discuss how every marriage with children needs the investment of time in the marriage relationship, which is the primary relationship in the family. You know the old saying: the best way to love my children is to love my spouse. So take stock of the six areas of need in every marriage with children and rate your standing:

1. *Balance:* When children enter a marriage, the whole relationship changes and seems to throw your feelings and focus and awareness of each other off balance. Have you regained a sense of balance in your relationship since children have become part of your lives?

2. *Commitment:* Throughout your marriage, you are challenged, to live out the "I do's" of your wedding vows. Commitment is not based on feelings, but is an intentional act of the will to live out your promises to each other. As parents, are you discovering what it means to stick together, even when it's not fun— through the flu, financial crises, unexpected moves, and meeting extended family needs?

3. *Interdependence:* A husband and wife each bring who they are individually to the marriage, and then realize how their separate parts affect their combined future. You are growing and changing together all

the time. Are you and your husband redefining who you are, now that you are mom and dad?

4. *Intimacy:* Most people assume that intimacy in marriage means sex, but it means more than that. It means "into me see." It means caring enough and taking the time to reveal your inner soul and heart to your spouse. Have you made room for romance and intimacy both sexually and personally since the arrival of your little one?

5. *Mission:* When you become parents, you start thinking about your values and the importance of passing those values on to your children. Do you know what makes your family a family? Have you taken the time to identify your values?

6. *Hope:* All of us get stuck sometimes in the darkness of the moment, wondering if there will ever be a light at the end of the tunnel. Hope is that light. Hope gives us something to look forward to. Hope is knowing that what we see now is not all there is. Can you envision a new meaning for "happily ever after"?[9]

Marriage forms the foundation for partnering in your parenting. Do you need to shore up any parts of that foundation?

SEE "WHAT TO DO NEXT": GROWING YOUR MARRIAGE, PAGE 179.

The Rewards of Partnering

Partnering in parenting yields great rewards as mom and dad work together at the common goal of raising little ones to become competent, independent adults. The first reward is that *functioning as partners is much less tiring.* Writer Ruth Barton underlines, "God's instruction for us to attend to our children is huge and multifaceted, but when men and women are committed to it together, it is much less overwhelming."[10] When two attend to the parenting functions of diapering, driving, feeding, bathing, dressing, and disciplining, both find time and freedom for recovery and replenishment.

The second reward is that *partnering is wiser*. Dads and moms are different. Each brings unique skills and strengths as well as moments and places of weakness. Partnering pairs strengths with deficits and provides better parenting for the child.

And the third reward is that *partnering makes parenting more fun!* In his book *The Triumphant Marriage*, Neil Clark Warren describes this reward for parents. "When they take it on as partners, when they see what a sacred privilege it is, when they come to recognize that rearing great kids is a goal worth pursuing, they are headed toward something wonderful."[11]

Puppet or partner? Which will it be, mom? The answer comes in remembering what you can control and what you can't control; what you are responsible for, and what you are not. You can control yourself and your choices. But you cannot control your husband, and you are not responsible for his choices. You can, however, influence and encourage those choices.

SEE "WHAT TO DO NEXT": KEEP GROWING, PAGE 158.

Let's go back to the example of the mom and dad exiting the plane at the airport. In the first example, the mom controlled the dad's "strings," assuming she could manage him better than he could manage himself. In the second example, the mom let her husband have total control. Both are examples of puppeteering. Let's roll it back and see what partners might do as they exit the plane together.

In partnering, a couple is more mutual, and yet both mom and dad remain individuals. This time as the plane lands, dad picks up the diaper bag and the hoists the toddler son into his arms. As he turns toward the front of the plane, he looks over his shoulder for his wife, noting that she's carrying the baby in its infant seat. Mom maneuvers her purse, adjusts the baby's blanket, and then glances back at their seats for any forgotten toys or other possessions.

All set. Dad and mom move together down the aisle of the plane and then exit into the jetway and the airport. At the computer monitor, dad checks the gate for the next flight while mom converses with their excited toddler. Turning to dad she says, "Here, the baby's getting fussy. Can we switch?" Mom then takes the tickets and the toddler's hand from dad, and together they set off toward the next installment of their journey.

It doesn't matter who is carrying the baby here, who is leading, who is following, or who has the tickets. What matters is that both mom and dad are sharing the task of going in the same direction. They are mutually interested in helping each other and the children get to where they're going. Sometimes one steps back and lets the other take the lead. Sometimes it's the other way around. It's not about who's right and who's in control. It's about partnering.

The choice is ours. We certainly can survive as puppets, and we can even become expert at controlling and manipulating the strings of the lives of those around us. But at what price for ourselves, our husbands, and our children? It's time for the Pinocchios of our world to become real . . . and choose partnering.

Make Room for Reflection

- Do you identify with any of the mothers in the family trying to make a connecting flight at the airport? In what ways?

- Do you tend to take the role of puppet or puppeteer in your marriage? What forces influence this choice? How might you challenge yourself in this area?

- What aspects of partnering attract you? What issues make you uncomfortable?

- Think of an area where you are having trouble communicating your feelings to your husband in a way he understands. What word picture can you think of to describe your feelings, like the quarterback analogy in this chapter?

- Identify your expectations for your husband as a father. What does he do that you wish he didn't do? What doesn't he do that you wish he did? Where do you need to adjust your expectations to who this man really is? How would you approach going a step further to communicate your old and new expectations to him?

Top Tips about Pops from MOPS

- A few weeks ago, I began to notice a startling change in the atmosphere in our home. Suddenly, my husband and I were getting louder and louder, often to the point of yelling at our two preschoolers. My three-year-old daughter was reacting by getting louder and louder as well. I felt we were escalating the problem. My husband and I went out for a "date" and I explained calmly what I thought the problem was, implicating myself as well. He agreed, and since then the noise level in our house has decreased by at least 90 percent. In fact, we have found together that speaking words of discipline in a soft voice is much more effective than shouting.

- Every night when he is home, my husband usually tends to the needs of our oldest child—feeds dinner, bathes, changes diapers, puts on pajamas, and tucks in with prayer—while I nurse and bathe the baby. While he puts our oldest to bed, I tidy up the kitchen. Good teamwork!
- I suggested that my husband could care for our infant daughter even when she is fussy—that since I had recently nursed her, I was no more capable than he was to offer her comfort.
- When he runs errands, one of the children usually goes with him.
- When our daughter would fall down and get hurt, she would always want me. I started not running to her, and let my husband take over—it was very hard to not jump in.

part three Daddy Style

chapter seven

He's Not "Duh," He's Different

Early in my career as a mother, I learned an invaluable lesson. There is a mode of operation, entirely distinct from the more conventional "Mommy-Style," that is nevertheless a useful thing to have on hand. It is, as you have already guessed, "Daddy-Style."

Everyone is familiar with "Mommy-Style." This is the cozy, predictable sequence of events many of us remember from our own childhoods: lunch before dessert, nap before playtime, bath before bed. This is the kind of daily life that gives small children security and develops their self-control. It also keeps Mommy sane.

"Daddy-Style," however, is everything that happens when Mommy is not there and Daddy is. It is cookies at 11:30. It is a trip to Home Depot at noon because nobody seemed to want lunch anyway and Baby falls asleep in the shopping cart and isn't tired by the time Daddy gets them home so baby doesn't take a nap. It is roughhousing with "The Giant" on the floor until ten minutes past bedtime, and then somebody ends up crying. And nobody gets a bath. Any time.

There is nothing inherently dangerous about "Daddy-Style." It is merely a bit . . . unique. On my homecoming from the hospital, Baby #3 in arms, I was greeted at the door with a bouquet of red roses—in an empty breast-pump cylinder. This, dear ladies, is "Daddy-Style." I suppose it might seem perfectly appropriate, if one cannot find a vase, to put a bouquet of red roses in a breast-pump cylinder—if you are a Daddy.

My first recollection of "Daddy-Style" occurred when I was a little girl myself, on a trip with my two sisters and my own daddy. We were back in Summit Hill, Pennsylvania, where Daddy grew up and tromped all over the mountains. We had visited an old neighbor of

Daddy's—the woman who used to bake chocolate cakes and pies and cookies, and shared them with hungry looking little boys. And can you believe it? She had just baked a chocolate cake! And by golly, she shared her goodies with some hungry looking little girls and their Daddy.

Up to the hills we went, with chocolate cake, still warm, and a quart of milk from the corner store. A blanket spread, little girls with grubby hands seated, and Daddy says, "Here's lunch!" His great grin, our wide and incredulous eyes, and a huge chunk of chocolate cake put in our palms. "Eat up! That's lunch!"

(Who can foresee what small event will impact a child's heart? That piece of cake was a taste of my father's boyhood—a bridging of decades in one big bite. Will I ever forget it?)

The wise Mommy learns to graciously accept any opportunity to let Daddy exhibit his Style. Go ahead and leave for a couple of hours! View your time away as a chance to regain perspective, to think a complete thought, to actually accomplish one item on your perpetual To Do List. Does that seem too selfish for a Mommy? All right then, try this. . . . Think of it as a way to develop your children's creative thinking skills: Does pancake syrup make mashed potatoes taste better? Does it make more sense to sleep in your clothes, so you're already dressed when you wake up tomorrow? Is there a way to play cards without any cards?

You will find that these doses of "Daddy-Style" are not only refreshing, but also answer some of the deep questions of your heart: Can a baby survive an hour of being snapped backwards into her footie pajamas? Will dancing to jazz before bedtime help toddlers fall asleep faster? Will children believe that the chicken burned in the microwave is really chicken jerky? Without "Daddy-Style," you might never find out.

So relax, Moms! After all, it won't be long until you're home again, putting everything back to normal: lunch before dessert, nap before playtime, bath before bed. All that security is great for kids. But so is a little bit of adventure! A little bit of . . . Daddy-Style!

—Amy Imbody, "Daddy-Style"

Moms and dads are different.

Duh.

But in living this out as parents, we sometimes get confused. Or competitive. Or controlling.

The fact is moms and dads parent their children differently. They give love differently. Call it maternal and paternal instinct, but moms and dads act different. Among the commonly accepted stereotypes are these: a mom pulls a baby in closely and nurtures the child next to her heart; dad lifts the baby high in the air. Mom is interested in the child's happiness; dad wants the child to be successful.

Take this recent Saturday morning scene in the waiting room of a pediatrician's office. Mom after mom enters with a diaper bag slung over one shoulder. Each confidently carries her baby in an identical fashion—kind of perched on a hip so she is face-to-face with the child. Then in comes a dad. Same confident stride. Same diaper bag slung over his shoulder. But he carries the baby backwards, his arm around the baby's tummy so that instead of facing father, the baby faces outwards, looking at the world. This backwards baby bobbles along happily as father and child approach the desk to sign in.

Here's the question: Is the baby backwards or is dad's style just different? And is mom's way better—or just different? Hmmm.

God made moms and dads different for a reason, and children need those differences as they grow up. Just as it takes both a sperm and an egg to conceive a child, it takes both kinds of love and both kinds of offerings in order for children to be balanced and whole. Newspaper columnist Leonard Pitts writes, "Allow me to state the obvious: men and women are different. They tend to communicate differently, prioritize differently, perceive and respond to the world differently.

Not better, not worse, but differently. In those differences lay the life lessons by which a boy or girl is rounded, shaped, taught how to be."[1]

It's easy to numbly accept those differences. Like when we say, "Of course moms and dads are different," and then bury ourselves in the commonly accepted stereotypes, therefore avoiding any analysis or appreciation of those differences. Or it's easy to make too much of the differences and get just as stuck in staunch refusals to carry out certain tasks or act certain ways because we don't give any validity to the gender stereotypes. It's time to find some balance and set the record straight with some basic facts.

Men and Women Are Different

Indeed, men are different from us. Consider the differences between you and your husband. Maybe he likes to take chances. He drives ten miles above the speed limit and lets the gas gauge hover dangerously close to empty. You'd rather be safe than sorry. You drive five miles below the speed limit (except when you're on the way to Girls' Night Out, and then you take after your husband). You head for the gas station when the gauge gets much below half.

Your husband likes to sleep in total darkness. You like to leave a night light on in the bathroom. He's a night person. You're a morning person. He gave up drinking coffee. You can't face the morning without two cups. You like crossword puzzles. He doesn't. You like parties. He'd rather have a quiet evening at home. He leaves the toilet seat up. You don't! Some of these differences are due to personality type. But others are more gender related.

Understanding the differences between men and women is simple if you use this analogy, according to authors Bill and Pam Farrel, who combine efforts to write about this topic:

Men are like waffles and women are like spaghetti. When you look at a waffle, you see a collection of boxes separated by walls, symbolic of the way that men process life in boxes. Each box has room for one issue and one issue only, and a man typically lives in only one box at a time. When he's at work, he's at work; when he watches television, that's where he is, and he can ignore everything else around him. Social scientists call it compartmentalizing. As a result, men are problem solvers. They enter a box, size up the problem, and come up with a solution. They look for a bottom line and try to get to it as quickly as possible. They feel best about themselves when they are solving problems.

In contrast, women view life more like a plate of spaghetti, where all the noodles wrap around and touch and intersect with each other. Every thought and every issue is connected to every other thought and issue. Life is more of a process for women than men. This is why women are usually better at multitasking than men. Women can talk on the phone and stir the dinner on the stove while making notes for tomorrow's business meeting and opening the backdoor for her children. Because a woman's thoughts, emotions, and convictions are connected, she usually has a need to talk things through—it helps her to link together the logical, emotional, relational, and spiritual aspects of any given topic.

Men and women think differently, process emotions differently, make decisions differently, and learn differently. And yet they complement one another so beautifully that a healthy relationship increases their total offering.[2] Especially as they parent together. Here are some ways to begin to appreciate how dads are different.

SEE "WHAT TO DO NEXT": CAN YOU CHANGE YOUR HUSBAND? PAGE 178.

Dads Aren't "Duh"

Because our husbands parent *differently*, we sometimes think that they're "duh." That they don't get it; they're missing the obvious or important. That's too easy. When we assume they're "duh," we miss out on the unique and necessary offerings of their fathering. And so do our children.

Take the woman who found her husband standing over their baby's crib. Silently she watched him. As he stood looking down at the sleeping infant, she saw on his face a mixture of emotions: disbelief, doubt, skepticism. Touched by this unusual display of sensitivity, she slipped her arm around him. "A penny for your thoughts," she said, with eyes glistening. "It's amazing!" he replied. "I just can't see how anybody can make a crib like that for only $46.50."[3]

Truly! Amazing! This father thinks *differently* from his wife. But is he "duh"? Hardly. He obviously knew facts about construction, woodwork, supply prices, and the cost of labor she'd never considered.

Then there's the mom who greeted her baby one morning to find his diaper duct-taped together. She approached her husband about this inventive method for fastening a diaper, since he'd put the baby down the night before. He told her that they'd received a faulty box of diapers, and rather than waste them, he'd found a way to hold them in place with every man's solution to every household problem: duct tape! He'd even put the roll of tape and scissors in the changing table drawer, he told her proudly, to help them through the rest of the box of faulty diapers and middle-of-the-night emergencies. What a guy!

Such responses to the needs of children require creativity! Long ago, Dr. Benjamin Spock observed, "The more people have studied different methods of bringing up children, the more they have come to the conclusion that what good fathers feel like doing for their babies is the best after all."[4] Aha. This "knowing what to do with a baby" *is* instinctive for fathers just as it is for mothers. It's not that they don't have it; it's just that they do it differently. As one mom said, "Two plus two equals four, but so does three plus one."[5]

Dads Aren't Male Moms

Now this is big news, huh? To be honest, it is. As moms, we tend to think that fathering ought to look a lot like mothering, except that it's male. In our MOPS research, mom after mom reports that her husband is "too harsh," "impatient," "unfamiliar," or "not a good listener" when it comes to his fatherly duties. Instead, they want him to be more "under-

What Dads Say About...

WHAT DADS NEED MOST FROM YOU
(FROM DADS IN OUR SURVEY)

- Not to be so stressed and worried about everything.
- To observe my relationship with my son and strengthen it with words of praise and constructive feedback.
- Better understanding of my feelings.
- Positive words to the kids even when I'm not around.
- More appreciation for what I do for my kids.
- Not to air our different opinions in front of the kids, since that forces them to take sides.
- Not be the bad guy and handle all the discipline when I get home from work.
- Support and confidence in my abilities and judgment.
- Freedom to "goof off" with the kids sometimes and not worry so much about rigid schedules.
- A reminder of how my father was with me.
- Your prayers.

standing," "kind," "flexible," and "patient." They want him to father the way they mother.

As we discussed in chapter 2 in the section on the evolution of fatherhood, we've seen a shift from physically and emotionally distant fathers back towards a more hands-on style. Still, we are haunted by the remains of the view that held fathers to be auxiliary. In the book *The Faith Factor in Fatherhood,* Wade Horn identifies three myths that have contributed to the decline of fatherhood in our country:

1. The myth of the androgyny model. In the 1960s, social psychologists began teaching that sex roles were interchangeable and that it made no difference how a child was reared. The androgynous father has become a feminized and weak parent.
2. The myth of the superfluous father. After the father became feminized, the role became irrelevant. A father was seen as just another mother.
3. The myth of the resilient child. The view that children can easily overcome the trauma of divorce further underlined the view that fathers were unimportant since most children of divorce reside with their mothers and do fine.[6]

Men aren't male mothers; they will parent differently than women. In the arena of play, the differences are obvious. Research by Dr. Michael Lamb of the University of Michigan in Ann Arbor indicates that dads are more "physical in their play than are mothers. They bounce and lift their babies, especially their sons. And while mothers typically talk to their infants and play with toys in a conventional manner, fathers are more likely to jostle and lightly roughhouse without toys. When they do play with objects, they use them in unique and more creative ways than their wives do."[7] *Today Show* host Al

Roker testifies to this difference in his parenting saying, "I think that in general I let [my daughter] be sillier. I like to be silly with her. I think dads let babies take more of a risk, maybe bounce off a bed more or jump off a couch or do more risk-taking things."[8]

SEE "WHAT TO DO NEXT": HOW TO HELP HIM CONNECT WITH HIS KIDS, PAGE 169.

There are other areas where fathers parent differently than mothers. Moms in our survey report a father's tendency to discipline misbehavior more quickly, using a harsher tone of voice, but also using more creativity in interpreting the house "rules," even making "games" out of daily duties. Here's a sampling of some other comments from moms about the differences:

- I'm the dinner and he's the dessert. They get their nourishment from me, but at the end of the day, he's what they look forward to.
- He's more daring than I am with our children. He takes our five-year-old biking. If it was me, she'd still be using training wheels.
- He's a stricter disciplinarian. When I get soft from being with them all day, he brings us back to balance.
- He's better helping with sick children than I am.
- He is better able to fix things than I am.

When we make fathers into male mothers, we lose their unique offering, which our children need.

Dads Aren't All Alike

Just as men aren't male mothers, neither are all fathers alike. Differences in personality and style abound within the parameters of fathering. This list of "Special Dad Traits" appeared anonymously in a local newsletter around Father's Day. As you read through it, you may realize that yours may not match up with all these stereotypes, which just goes to prove that dads aren't all alike.

Some Things That Make Dads Special
- Can be showered and ready in ten minutes.
- Know useful stuff about tanks and airplanes.
- Can open all jars and kill own food.
- Think that flowers and duct tape can fix everything.
- Can watch two back-to-back Sunday afternoon football games.
- One mood, all the time.
- Phone conversations usually last thirty seconds.
- Five-day vacation requires one suitcase.
- Wake up as good-looking as they went to bed.

You probably get the picture. Just as moms don't like the stereotyping of "good moms always _____" (fill in the

BABY BLUES®

Reprinted with special permission of King Features Syndicate.

blank with your own pet peeves), neither do dads. Different personalities make for different dads. One dad may insist on attending preschool parent-teacher conferences, while another rejoices with complete satisfaction at the finger-painting displayed on the fridge and needs no more indication of his child's prowess. One dad stands on the sidelines at the soccer game yelling out instructions for every play, while another wouldn't think of offering any coaching and distracts himself with a bag of popcorn. One dad likes to make up stories at bedtime; another asks where the library books are.

SEE "WHAT TO DO NEXT": THE LEGACY OF LOVE, PAGE 181.

In his book *Women Are Always Right and Men Are Never Wrong,* Joey O'Connor wonders if women have any idea of what *really* happens when mom goes away for the weekend: "So far, wives only have general ideas of what goes on all

weekend (true) and that the only meals that kids eat are cereal and Happy Meals (true) and that several near-accidents involving hot waffle irons and fingers, broken glass, snail poison, and climbing on the roof are narrowly averted (all true), but if wives ever really found out what happens with Dad and the kids when they're away, WOOHOO, boy, would that unpack their bags!"[9]

Okay? He's not "duh." He's different. Different from you and different from other dads you know. This is a *good* thing! One sociologist underlines the benefits of two *different* parents in an intact family this way: "When both parents are present, they can play different, even contradictory, roles. One parent may goad the child to achieve, while the other may encourage the child to take time out to daydream or toss a football around. One may emphasize taking intellectual risks, while the other may insist on following the teacher's guidelines.[10]

One may tenderize. The other may toughen. One may teach while the other listens. One may play and the other hold. Both love. Acknowledge the differences between mom and dad and then celebrate the offering you each bring in your life and in the life of your child.

Make Room for Reflection

- Take an honest look at how you view your responsibility in parenting. Which portrayal fits you?
    - 50/50 partner with your husband
    - 100 percent responsible for parenting, with your husband as helper
    - Responsible to be the helper to your husband's role of being 100 percent responsible

While there are many other possible options, these reveal a bit about our thinking. Going back to the concept of puppet or partner, where do you think the responsibility for parenting should lie in your marriage? What does your view of the style of your husband's fathering say about whether you think he is "duh" or just different?

- See your differences as opportunities to get to know each other better. Relationships thrive when people respect each others' differences and give each other the freedom to do things their own way. With this in mind, name five ways you and your husband parent similarly. Now name five ways you parent differently.

- Name three adjectives that describe your personality. Your child's? Your husband's? What are some ways in which your husband's personality complements yours?

- Name three specific ways you can celebrate the differences in personality and parenting styles you've just identified.

Top Tips about Pops from MOPS

- Every time my husband grabs his tools to do a minor fix-it job around the house, I find my sons' play tools so they can "help."
- I brag about my husband to other people when he is present.
- I try to never criticize when he helps. Maybe the kids' clothes don't match, or their hair isn't combed, but I appreciate his help.
- I ask my husband how I can help him.

chapter eight

Understanding
Original Differences

If you are a mom, like I am, you probably have some very vivid memories of being awakened in the middle of the night by insistent cries for a warm bottle. Although this is our third child, the nocturnal ritual of parenthood has not become any easier. As I lay comfortably in my bed dreaming of ... oh, I don't know ... sleep perhaps, somewhere around the fringes of my conscious I hear the soft whimpers of our son as be begins to wake up. I don't have to look at the clock. I know by now that it is exactly 3:23 A.M. I hold my breath, inwardly whispering a prayer, "Please God, let him sleep through the night." My prayer goes unanswered. The whimper turns to a full-scale howl. I feel in the darkness for my slippers, my robe. My husband rouses and then goes back to sleep. I sigh. It must be nice ... to get sleep. As I warm the baby's bottle, I think about how quiet the house is, how still. It's as if everything and everyone everywhere is sleeping. Everyone except for Emmanuel ... and me.

The crying has stopped. I wonder if he has fallen asleep. As silently as possible I approach his door. Unexpectedly, I see my husband, gently rocking and comforting our little son. I pause for a moment not wanting to interrupt their exchange. My husband looks up and sees me. He smiles. "See, Mommy has your bottle," he says.

Although I feel exhausted, I reach to take the baby from his arms. "I'll feed him," he tells me. "You get some rest."

I really want to take him up on that, but I know he's tired too. I don't have the chance to protest. Father and son have settled into a chair beside the baby's crib. They are talking about warm bottles and how everything is all right.

Resting again comfortably in my bed, I hear the sound of gentle kisses as the baby sucks away on the bottle. I feel the soundless smile. I think to myself, "This is what love and family are all about." I am thankful for my babies and for so many things. But at this moment, I am most thankful for this man who continues to show me what love is all about.

Emmanuel has finished his bottle. My husband is back in bed. I rest my head against his shoulder. He wraps his arms around me. Everything is quiet and still. And soon we have all gone back to sleep.

—Hope Hèléne Murphy, "A Daddy Moment"

Most marriages aren't made up of just two individuals. They are made up of six people—husband plus wife, plus both their parents. In some cases the marriage is made up of even more folks, due to stepparents or significant others.

Such a combination of personalities and perspectives affects our mothering and fathering as well as our parenting together. As we journey along toward understanding daddy style and its uniqueness from mommy style, let's take a detour to examine the differences between you and your husband due to your families of origin—the mom and dad who parented you, how their style shaped you into the mom you are today, and the expectations about the father your children should have.

Just below the surface of our daily interactions is our "stuff." Our "stuff" is the baggage or influence we carry in our hearts and souls as a result of our histories. Each of us has developed certain ideas about how life should be lived as a mom or dad, and as mom and dad together, based on how we were raised. Most of the time these beliefs stay hidden somewhere deep inside. We aren't really aware of them until something triggers a response, and then one comes exploding out of our souls in a moment of stress or a difference of opinion.

In reality, our "stuff" shapes most of our responses in life, including the way we parent.

You may have noticed your parenting "stuff" at your baby's first Christmas. Though you had worked out a Christmas celebration with extended family in previous years, in this first year as parents yourselves, you are surprised by your differences. You have conflicting opinions about the number of presents a child should receive, or when and how they are opened. Or maybe you're surprised by your husband's absorption with the baby's presents rather than with the baby. Or maybe you disagree on the priority of meeting children's needs in the midst of his mother's formal family dinner. You make it through the day and night, but looking back, you can see your "stuff" sticking out all over that holiday memory. Expectations like "Christmas is about relationships" or "Christmas is about Jesus" haunt you as you process the discord of your holiday. *What was that about?* you wonder.

It might be that you notice your stuff when your child begins to require discipline. As your toddler reaches toward the space heater, your husband catches her and smacks her hand. Your instinct is to merely move her out of the danger. You are shocked that he hits her. Out comes your stuff about discipline, which grew out of your own experiences of being disciplined harshly as a child, and you unleash your anger at your husband.

Some moms may feel a bit threatened to examine and talk about this original family stuff. The truth is, it's just plain helpful. When we dig beneath our expectations for ourselves as a mom or our husband as a dad, we gain understanding as to the origins of those expectations, and we're better able to deal with any issues that affect our parenting. In the process, we also discover what really matters to us and why. Such understanding will help us as women, as wives, and as moms.

Understanding "Stuff"

In her book *Necessary Losses*, Judith Viorst writes, we "bring into marriage the unconscious longings and the unfinished business of childhood, and prompted by the past, we make demands in our marriage, unaware of what we do."[1] Okay. That's the stuff we're talking about. Just as the heart longings we discussed earlier shape our expectations for our husbands as fathers, so does the stuff of how we ourselves were raised.

One mom reports, "Sometimes it's hard because I do compare him to my father, who was very loving and sensitive. He knew how to interact with little kids. My husband was an only child, and he's not quite sure how to act with little ones—especially girls—so he teases, tickling, chasing, sticking his finger in their ears, etc. The girls tire of it and ask him to stop, and he doesn't know when to quit . . . I just want him to hold them without teasing."

Perhaps you were raised by a single mom. Okay—the absence of a father may have shaped you to withdraw from conflict or, contrastingly, to stand strong and independently at all costs, which affects how you expect your husband to father. If you were raised with a loving, involved father, your assumptions regarding your husband's fathering may lead you to expect him to mirror what you had in a father. Further, your husband's experience with his parents influences how he lives out his own role as a parent. He may resist diaper changing if that was a chore his father avoided as "women's work." Or he might slip into a work-centered lifestyle, handling his discomfort with the newness of fathering the way his father handled his: by leaving.

As we said in the previous chapter, moms and dads parent differently. Sometimes the differences are due to gender or personality. In other moments, the differences arise out of the stuff of how each of you were raised. Understanding how such stuff shapes us is extremely helpful as we seek to be partners in parenting. Let's separate out our thinking into our individual stuff: hers and his.

SEE "WHAT TO DO NEXT": HIDDEN STUFF IN YOUR HEART, PAGE 155.

Her Stuff

The two obvious sources of stuff in your life are your mom and your dad. How you were parented by each affects how you mother and how you influence your husband's fathering.

Gender roles are a huge influence. Your mother's role in your original family shapes yours in your family today. Most likely, you either mirror her role or contrast it. If she was loving and nurturing, you probably have done the important work of integrating some aspects of her mothering into your style while intentionally separating from others. If your mother lacked in some of her mom skills, you've probably invented ways to survive and grow on your own.

Similarly, the role of your dad in your upbringing is not only crucial to your mothering today, it greatly affects your expectations of your husband as a father. As H. Norman Wright summarizes in his book *Always Daddy's Girl: Understanding Your Father's Impact on Who You Are*, "Your father is still influencing your life today—probably more than you realize. For example, your present thoughts and feelings about yourself and your present relationships with other men reflect your father's impact on you. So often, what a father *gives* to his daughter affects her expectations toward the men in her life. Similarly, what a father *withholds* from his daughter can also affect her expectations toward other men."[2]

A healthy relationship with your father leads you to desire for your husband to repeat the offering in the lives of your children; as this mom points out, "I vividly remember my father being interested and involved in our school and other activities. Our children haven't reached school age, but it will be hard to live up to my father's level of involvement." Another mom writes, "My father was involved in the housework, grocery shopping. . . . I would like my husband to model that more for my children so they wouldn't see housework as just the woman's role." Still another writes, "I try to tell him how my dad was with me and ask him to be more like that, but it's hard to take that kind of advice from me. And I'm sure that I make him feel bad, but I want my kids to have the kind of relationship I had with my dad."

When our dads *didn't* do it "right," we can bring all kinds of expectations to our husbands to "make up for it" in the lives of our little ones. One mom says, "While my dad has fond memories of my childhood, I remember him being authoritarian and withdrawn from the actual work of raising children."

Another reports, "I learned through some hard times how important a father figure is in a woman's life. I am thirty-two and still long to have a relationship with my daddy. My husband knows how important it is to start a relationship with his girls at a very young age in order to have one in the teenage and older years of their lives. I melt inside when they want their daddy instead of their mommy because I know there is already a special bond started." Still another mom writes, "My father emotionally abused us our whole lives. He would blow up and have enormous fits of rage over minor things. My husband is not like that at all. He is completely opposite with our kids, showing and telling them constantly how much he loves them."

If you are not sure about your father's impact on your life, Christian counselor H. Norman Wright suggests writing out a list of both your father's positive and negative qualities.

Some common answers to those questions from women included these positive responses:

- He's affectionate, supportive, and thinks about what is best for the family.
- My father is self-disciplined, responsible. He has grown to show his deep feelings of love for family. He tries to be more understanding and allow for two-way thought and conversation. Family priorities are first.
- He is compassionate, goal-oriented, tender, godly, loving, communicative, understanding, gentle, loving, a figure-outer of things.

Ambivalent responses included this one:

- My dad is very achievement-oriented. I haven't decided if that is positive or negative. . . . When I was growing up I never saw him. . . . I don't feel like I know my father very well and I can't really think of positive or negative qualities.

Negative comments included these:

- He is not a good listener. Sometimes too much of a Pollyanna, avoiding conflict. . . . He does not understand the emotional side of people very well.
- He isn't very good at money management.
- He has a bad temper and yells sometimes.
- He drinks too much.
- He is a successful workaholic.
- He gives conditional support, and uses mother as total communication mediator.
- He is controlling.[3]

Do any of these descriptions sound familiar to you? If you can think of your own list of positive and negative qualities about your mom and dad, you are apt to become more aware of your stuff as it relates to your mothering and your expectations about your husband's fathering. Consider the values passed on by both your mother and father. Think about how both your met and your unmet needs influence your expectations for just how you want your husband to father. These are some of the original family issues that continue to be part of who you are.

SEE "WHAT TO DO NEXT": PRACTICING FORGIVENESS, PAGE 156.

His Stuff

According to our survey, about 70 percent of dads report that they see themselves as being different or very different from their fathers and 94 percent are pleased by these differences. That's an amazing statistic. It means plain and simple that even if today's dads are dissatisfied with the fathering they received as children, they want to insure that their children have a better experience.

But being dissatisfied and wanting to be different doesn't always mean knowing what to do about it. As one father in our survey said, "We need more models of what a good father is. The only models we have are our own fathers. Isn't that scary!"

Some moms responding to our questionnaire gave their reflections on how the fathering their husbands received affects the way they father: "My husband has a difficult time because he has no father of his own to model after. At a young age he was placed in a children's home (like an orphanage) and never had a personal model to imitate. He certainly can use more knowledge and encouragement about fathering." Another mom comments, "My husband didn't have a father that was home a lot, so he didn't see that as important. He feels the father's role is simply to provide for the family. His grandfather walked out on his father's family when the children were young so my husband's father didn't know how to be a father. That has started a pattern of not being there for your children on my husband's side of the family."

Another mom describes the way she attempts to help her husband overcome the ways in which he was fathered: "His own father was an alcoholic. He was the seventh of ten children and never had the quality time he needed with his own father . . . so I try to involve my husband in every activity that the kids get involved in."

This all-too-common experience creates a sort of father hunger which is enormous for both men and women. Maybe these fathers were absent. Maybe they were simply passive and emotionally uninvolved, but when we miss out on the blessing of a father in our daily lives, we are forever influenced.

How your husband was mothered also affects his fathering—and his interaction with you as the mother of his children. Brenda Hunter reports, "If a man had a mother who was physically or emotionally absent for most of his childhood . . . he will most likely not know what emotional closeness or intimacy feels like. So how can he possibly know what his child is missing?"[4] And once again, in the reverse, if his mother met his needs, he will relate differently both to you and to his children.

In his book *Real Boys,* Dr. William Pollack writes about the power of mothers in their sons' lives:

> Mothers help make boys into men. Far from making boys weaker, the love of a mother can and does actually make boys stronger, emotionally and psychologically. Far from making boys dependent, the base of safety a loving mother can create—a connection that her son can rely on all his life—provides a boy with the courage to explore the outside world. But

most important, far from making a boy act in "girl-like" ways, a loving mother actually plays an integral role in helping a boy develop his masculinity—the self-esteem and strength of character he needs to feel confident in his own masculine self.[5]

SEE "WHAT TO DO NEXT": CAN YOU CHANGE YOUR HUSBAND? PAGE 178

Both the good and not-so-good influences from our past can be understood. The good can be used for good, and the woundedness can be overcome. But our experience in the past still shapes our expectations in the present as we parent. When we bring these hidden expectations—and their origins—out into the light, we have more to offer in our roles as moms and dads.

Make Room for Reflection

Understanding how our early experiences with our fathers affect the way we parent today can help us weed out our fathers' bad influences on our parenting and foster the good. In *The Father Book,* three psychologists offer a helpful series of questions to help us pinpoint those influences. Answer the following questions to gain insight into your own needs as well as those of your husband.

1. What are your memories of how your father felt toward you? Good? Angry? Indifferent? Mention a specific memory that led you to feel this way.

2. In way ways did your dad punish (that is, discipline) you?

   • Physical contact: spanking, slapping, swatting, shaking.

   • Verbal: yelling, belittling, mocking, name-calling, chewing out.

   • Tactical: removing privileges, grounding, forcing behaviors such as sitting in a certain chair or standing in a corner.

3. Of these methods, from the viewpoint of adulthood, which do you think were the most effective in keeping you in the straight and narrow? Which ones didn't really work on you?

4. How did you feel when you walked into a room where he was, or when he walked into a room where you were?
   - Glad he came in?
   - Indifferent?
   - A little uneasy?
   - You could feel anger or resentment stirring.
   - Other

5. How do you feel now as an adult when that happens?
   - Glad to see him?
   - Indifferent?
   - A little uneasy?
   - You can feel anger or resentment stirring.
   - Other

6. What are some positive events you remember with your dad (attendance at sporting events, activities such as working on the car, goof-off things, or one-on-one family outings)?

7. What are some negative events (an activity or event he promised you and had to renege on; things you intensely wished he'd do and he did not; trips or activities that went sour; times you screwed up or he did; times he caught you when you were up to no good, or others ratted on you; an occasion in which you discovered him in something he shouldn't be doing)?

8. As you look at the specific events above from an adult perspective, how might common fears have been influencing your father's actions and attitudes?
   - Fear of being outshone
   - Fear of messing up
   - Fear of the unknown
   - Fear of being denied respect or losing respect[6]

Top Tips about Pops from MOPS

- I try every day to compliment my husband so that our children hear.
- I work nights, so I encourage daddy-daughter time while I do my thing.
- I try not to set up stereotypes of what a father or mother should do. We just work to get it all done together.
- When discussing my father's most recent visit, I thanked my husband for not being the kind of dad that my dad was. I let him know that I am thankful that he is our children's daddy. I also told him that I'm almost jealous of the lifelong relationship he is forming with them, as I've never had that with my dad.
- I told my husband that if I hadn't had such a wonderful father, I would be wishing he was my father.

chapter nine

Dealing
with the Differences

Ever since we've been married, I've wanted my husband to do things my way. Why? Because I assume my way is better.

Take the way we swallow pills, for instance.

I put a pill into my mouth, take a sip of water, and swallow.

He puts a pill into his mouth and whiplashes his head backwards in order to swallow. It's some weird habit he learned in childhood. Obviously, an "original family issue."

"You don't need to do it that way," I tell him . . . but what I really mean is, "Do it my way because my way is better."

I'm sure this attitude has spilled over into other areas of our lives together . . . like mothering and fathering.

Why do I think my way is better? I don't have a good answer . . . so maybe I need to think about that question some more.

—Carol Kuykendall

Just the other day, I listened as my husband initiated our sixteen-year-old daughter to the wonders of cell phone technology. Now that she is driving, we both want her to have one for emergencies.

"Dad, how do I record a message?"

"Let me check the book and then I'll tell you."

"No, I want to do it myself."

She moved toward the book, but he steered it out of her grasp and continued reading.

"Whatever!" she proclaimed and huffed back to her room.

I wouldn't have done it that way, I thought. *I'd have asked my daughter to look up the instructions in the book and follow them, so that she could get a feel for how the information was detailed in the book. That's the way my mom did it. He did it wrong, I mused. He missed out on a great fathering moment.*

Five minutes later, I hear my husband knocking softly on our daughter's closed door and her invitation to enter. He moved her through the steps. She giggled and recorded her voice. And then for a full ten minutes, they doubled over in laughter as they scrolled through the musical ring selections.

However he did "it," I recognized, it worked. No, it wasn't the way I'd do it. But I'm not my daughter's father. I'm her mom.

—**Elisa Morgan**

We now recognize that dad's not "duh," he's different. Further, we know some of the reasons why he's different. Now comes the question, How are we going to deal with the differences? Let's look at several answers.

Some Moms Interfere

We asked moms how they respond to their husband's fathering when it is different from their mothering, and we got honest confessions like these:

- When he is explaining something to my son, I butt in and do the explaining.
- I often interfere . . . my mouth engages before my brain kicks in.
- I nag him too much.
- I need to be more patient with him.
- I need to encourage more and criticize less.
- I need to be less critical, but it's hard to change.

Time after time, moms admitted interfering and correcting when it comes to their husbands' fathering. What are the reasons behind this behavior? Moms admit it's because they are tired, too busy, too stressed, too critical, and too much of a control freak and perfectionist. Here are some of their quotes:

- It's hard to accept someone's parenting style when it's different from all you've grown up with.
- It's easier for me to do the chores in the interest of time.
- Sometimes I don't want to lose control over the kids. It doesn't occur to me that his way of handling a situation could be just as wonderful, only different than my way.
- It's hard to change.
- I don't know. Maybe because my own emotions get in the way a lot.

What do the men think of this? When asked what they need most from their wives in order to be good dads, we got answers like these:

- Encouragement without criticism.
- Support and affirmation.
- Encouragement and patience.
- Encouragement and understanding.
- Encouragement and freedom to goof around.
- Encouragement and good communication.

So why do we interfere when we know we shouldn't, and know that dads don't like it? Let's look deeper into the motivations that move us to interfere so often.

We Think Our Way Is Better

This attitude is an extension of the Mother Superior posture. Moms are the experts on kids. We know best. In fact, we know better than anyone else. Our way of displaying this attitude is by interfering. Why allow dad to do it wrong when we can fix it or correct it and keep it right?

And here comes that little desire for control again. Control is a tough issue to recognize in a marital relationship or in a parenting setting. But when we turn this control issue around and view it from a child's perspective toward an intrusive parental authority over them, we see the control issue more clearly. Imagine how you might have felt if your own mother was overbearingly critical, always correcting and intrusive.

Judith Viorst helps us understand this kind of mother-child control.

> An intrusive mother does for us what we want to, ought to, need to do for ourselves, rushing in to monitor our every breath and act, rushing in to wipe us and wash us and warn us, rushing in to prop up our castle before the blocks tumble down and to finish our words before they're out of our mouth, rushing in to assist and correct and protect us. Hovering so ceaselessly and anxiously, she challenges our conviction that, yes indeed, we can make it on our own. Unable to relinquish us, or her power over us, she insists on controlling all aspects of our experience.[1]

Such "helpful edits" can now be seen for what they are: interfering intrusions into another person's choices. When we assume that we know better, we imply that no one else knows as much as we do. How powerless we leave those we love! When, in fact, we long to set our children and loved ones free and place ourselves in the direction of freedom, we instead trap everyone with our pretense of indispensability and superior knowledge. No one can make a move without us. We pay a price for those controlling choices, however. One mom who's learned the hard way remarks, "I made the mistake of putting our daughter beside me instead of her father when we eat dinner. Now, I am responsible for feeding her all the time, so when everyone else is done eating, I am just getting started." Another mom recognizes the pattern she's fallen into and admits, "I'm too critical about little things and get into a pattern of nit-picking."

Perhaps Laura Doyle has a point in her popular book, *The Surrendered Wife*. She describes how she gave up trying to tell her husband what to do and how to do it, and how that greatly improved their relationship. Such advice is aimed at enhancing a marriage, but is applicable to fathering and child-care as well. The idea is to give a man the space and respect to follow his own best judgment, without interfering.

Still, we resist. When forced to face the truth, many moms agreed with the one who wrote, "I have always been the main caregiver. Sometimes it's hard to give up that control."

We Don't Think He Knows How

By now it may have dawned on us that our husband parents differently than we do, yet many of us still doubt that his "differences" will translate into the right stuff to meet the needs of our children. Will he figure out how to shampoo and rinse a toddler's hair without stinging her eyes in the process? Can he make mac and cheese the way a picky eater likes it? One mom admits, "Since I'm the one who is home with the children the majority of the time, I just have a routine and way of doing things, and I think sometimes it's hard for me to admit someone else could do it a different way and yet just as effectively."

In his work with the National Center for Fathering, Ken Canfield surveyed men and discovered that indeed "a lack of know-how" is one of the major barriers men face as fathers.[2] There is clearly a learning curve for dads, just as there is for us as moms. Knowing how to bathe a baby is not instinctive; it must be learned. While we may have accepted this fact for ourselves, we may overlook that reality in our husbands. They will need to learn to father through experience just as we need to learn to mother.

We Think He's Too Harsh

Another clear-cut reason we interfere with our husband's fathering is that we think he's too harsh. He seems mean sometimes. He doesn't encourage cooperation from a child; he demands it. His voice isn't soft and sweet; it's deep and sometimes way too loud. And when he settles a squabble, he might use physical force, not psychological bartering. He doesn't seem sensitive to the child's feelings.

We get uncomfortable with such an approach. Why? Most likely the experience we had with our own fathers plays a role. Were you nervous around your dad—even a bit afraid? You might be bringing that response into your reaction to your husband's fathering. Other forces also play a role, such as any relationships we've had with men: boyfriends, teachers, bosses, others.

Because of this concern, we can do crazy things. Take this mom for example. She commented, "If our son hurts himself, I will take him away from his father to comfort him, even though I know our son doesn't mind who is holding him."

While there just might be good reasons for an occasional interference in our husband's fathering, constantly editing and correcting, intruding and interrupting, sabotages his success and confidence as a father. Dealing with your husband's differences from you as a parent means identifying those patterns of interference and moving from interfering to informing.

Informing versus Interfering

Guess what? Most dads are scared to death about many aspects of fathering. Excited and thrilled at the prospect of parenting, they realize, "Hey, nobody's ever taught me how to do this!" Where training was an integral part of any occupation they've ever undertaken, men come into fathering without so much as a manual. As Ken Canfield puts it, "Fathering skills don't automatically accompany the Y chromosome your dad gave you."[3]

Mom, you can impact and influence your husband's fathering by recognizing his need for information and by refraining from interfering. Encourage him instead, by taking on a posture of being honest and informing. One dad described how this attitude helped him. "Bringing home our baby was like bringing home china. I didn't know what to do and my wife seemed to fall into it so naturally. I felt like an idiot. . . . It seemed like I was always stumbling. Then she told me that she didn't know what she was doing either, and that made me feel a lot better. But she seemed to have a natural way with the baby. She coached me on a few things, like holding, burping, and changing."[4]

Here are several ways you can move from interfering to informing.

Help him by being honest about your own needs to learn about parenting. Just as the dad above describes, his wife's honesty about her inadequacies freed him to be more open to learning what he needed to know. Admit your own needs and the ways you are seeking to learn about parenting too.

Help him see fathering as "work." Men understand work. They're born and bred to bring home the bacon or the bread or the Boboli. When you help your child's father understand that being a good father means mastering certain parenting skills, just as being a good employee means following certain procedures, you're communicating in a world he understands.

SEE "WHAT TO DO NEXT": HOW TO HELP HIM CONNECT WITH HIS KIDS, PAGE 169.

Help him attend to his children. Many men aren't into the details. They're more big picture, as this mom comments: "I am more in tune with the kids needs. . . . For example, if I am sick and have to stay in bed (which doesn't usually happen), he will do okay in taking the kids out of the room, taking them downstairs, and putting on a movie, but he might forget about the fact that the kids need food simply because he's not hungry."

Another mom says, "I think he is often times too tired to give the children the attention they sometimes need, so as a distraction he puts on the TV. Although he will sit with them, I wish he was more energetic and could actually do more things with them."

Children need attention in two main areas: (1) general development and (2) specific personality. Help your husband understand that he needs to consider both areas in order to father well. Give him some basic descriptions of what to expect developmentally of his child at her specific age. Then, teach your husband to watch for and learn about the unique personality characteristics of his child. Is she shy or outgoing? Athletic or artistic? A dreamer or a doer? Help him notice the smaller details and respond to them.

SEE "WHAT TO DO NEXT": HOW TO HELP HIM UNDERSTAND CHILD DEVELOPMENT, PAGE 174.

Help him love his children. Without exception, every child needs to be loved and nurtured. It is the relationship with both mom and dad which serves as a launching pad for the child's future growth. When discipline must be given, it achieves its purpose only when it is extended from a relationship of love. "A nurturant, encouraging father reaches out; he is proactive in offering affirmation or comfort; he takes the initiative in giving recognition. 'In you I am well pleased,' he communicates. He tapes the crudely colored crayon drawing on his office wall. He doesn't fly into a rage when a report card has mostly B's instead of A's."[5]

Many men struggle with offering love to their children because they did not experience their own fathers as loving. Fathering has evolved from the emotionally distant, breadwinner model of years past to the warmer and more nurturing fathers of today. But many men need encouragement to give this kind of love because they themselves did not experience it growing up.

Help your husband learn to listen for his child's feelings. Encourage him to show his pride in their accomplishments and character, and to demonstrate his love through hugs and playtime.

SEE "WHAT TO DO NEXT": HOW TO HELP HIM HEAR YOUR ADVICE, PAGE 168.

Help him by affirming him. We all appreciate affirmation and encouragement. Dads are no exception. The more supported they feel by their wives, the more confidence men express in their fathering. So affirm his efforts, even (and especially) when you recognize that you have criticized unfairly, as this mom describes: "One time when I left the kids at home with Dad, he took them to town for lunch. I criticized him for spending the money on going out when there was plenty of food in the refrigerator. He told me that he never gets the opportunity to take his kids out and treat them to something as simple as French fries. He was right."

GOOD ADVICE AND HOW TO GIVE IT

(FROM DADS IN OUR SURVEY)

- She communicates about issues with our kids—what is going right and wrong—so we can build a common strategy.

- She builds me up and never talks negatively about me to our children.

- She's pushy in the right way at the right times.

- She keeps me informed on her readings about the new ideas being done for children in childrearing.

- She reminds me of important dates and events.

- She points out when I create expectations that are not obtainable at the children's age levels.

- She tells me how much my daughter loves me.

- She doesn't watch over me while I am with our son.

- She has the kids visit me at work or make little art projects for me and pray for me when I am gone during the day.

- She doesn't "dump" the kids on me when I get home from work. This used to be a problem, but we have resolved it by giving me some down time when I get home. I afford her the same when she returns home from being gone.

- She doesn't pick apart the way I do things with our child.

- She makes sure there is excitement about my arriving home.

- She listens to my complaints and concerns. She does not brush me off and tell me to "act like a man," and that helps a lot!

- She reminds me that we need to have time together as husband and wife, not just "mom and dad."

Necessary Interference

In every mom-dad relationship there may come a moment when mom passionately feels that she must move from informing into interfering. We've spent the last few pages underlining the damage done when moms constantly inter-rupt their husband's fathering, and then offering principles for how to inform instead. But is interfering ever right?

Perhaps. But consider two principles before interfering. The first is *danger*. If your husband's actions or lack of actions might endanger your child, you must act. The second princi-ple which might require interference is *ignorance*. This second situation can usually be remedied by informing again. Say your husband walks in on your toddler, who is painting on the wall with thick, sloppy art paint. He does not know that you have given permission for this freedom since you are going to begin wallpapering that very wall shortly. Should you interfere with his poised and ready discipline? Yes, indeed, because he isn't aware of your permission.

One mom expresses her concerns this way, "I think the rules are too strict and that he's being too harsh. I really don't agree with the rules he sets, so I feel I can't honestly back him up." Like this mom, such moments of interference can be referred to as necessary.

When Dad Won't Be Dad

If you've read this far in this book, you really want dad to be dad. But what happens when dad won't be dad? There are dads who simply don't seem interested in fathering. They are distant and removed, uncaring and uninvolved. When this is the case, a mom has few options but to interfere and assume some of the fathering functions herself.

We've talked to moms who've expressed such concerns. Here are some of their descriptions:

- He works eighty hours in a week. He leaves before the kids get up and comes home after they go to bed. When he's home on the weekends, he feels that it is his time and doesn't want to be bothered.
- My husband doesn't ever clean up after himself. He is like another child. I have talked to him about counseling. He doesn't listen to anything I have to say.
- I am the full-time caretaker of our children. My husband used to be much more playful and enjoyed them more, but since we bought our home that seems to have become the most important thing to him. He feels this is the way he is and we need to accept it. It is hard for me; the kids are growing so fast and I love them so dearly. I can't understand how he doesn't feel the way I do, wanting to put them first.
- He is a workaholic who has little time for his family. He wants very little to do with parenting and leaves most decisions to me. He rarely makes time for the children, because he is gone 80 to 90 percent of the time. He is too tired to participate with us.

Here are some guidelines, intended to encourage you when dad won't be dad.

Keep in mind that people change. People change, even at eighty years old. Circumstances come which force us to reconsider our priorities and values. An illness. The loss of a job. A death. Even good times can cause us to pause. Just because the father of your children is not interested in fathering today doesn't mean that will define his involvement forever.

Keep praying. Prayer may not always change the circumstances, but it always changes us. When you hook yourself into the power of prayer on behalf of your husband, not only might he change, but you can change as well.

SEE "WHAT TO DO NEXT": PRAYING FOR YOUR KIDS' DAD, PAGE 194.

Remember that it's not your job to change him. It's his job to change himself. As Drs. Cloud and Townsend put it, maturity is when we are able to say, "My life is my problem." As long as you make his life your problem, he won't take it as his own.

We've said it is not your responsibility to change your husband, but in the book *What Husbands Wish Their Wives Knew about Men,* Patrick Morley offers this answer to the question, "What can I do to help my husband change?"

> The spiritual answer is that only God's grace can change a man, and you can best seek that through prayer. The practical answer is that he must be confronted in love with his sinful behavior. Perhaps you need some counseling to know how to do this. You will need to insist that he treat you respectfully as an expression of his duty to love and nurture you. If your husband is convicted of his sin and he changes, rejoice. If he doesn't immediately respond, continue in faith to help him gain self-control. Some of us are a little slow. One male counselor tells women, "I really feel for you having to live with us men. We are dense. If we haven't heard about it today, we think it must be fixed." Many husbands will not change. They are selfish and are not yet ready to submit to biblical principles of love and marriage. You must prepare yourself for that possibility. If your husband is not going to change, then you must learn how to cope. Don't let him pull you down. Don't be a codependent. In other words, don't let his problem become your problem. A codependent response would be if your husband wrongly gets mad and blames you, and you accept the blame. Don't let your difficult husband ruin your day.[6]

Realize that there's no such thing as a perfect family. It's easy to think that the family next door is happy-dappy and never struggles. We watch their minivan pull into their garage, the door slide down, and then we picture them safe inside enjoying family game night. Right. There is no such thing as a perfect family because families are human. And there is no such thing as a perfect Christian family, either. Christians are human as well. What makes them Christian is not some guarantee against struggle but rather the presence of Jesus with them in their struggles.

Understand that God can use their "imperfect" father in their lives. Children can succeed in spite of our failures. They can grow regardless of our inattention. And the fact is that they don't require only good times to grow; they can develop character, compassion, and insight from the harder periods of life as well. Having said this, if you need help, you need to get help. Your children will most likely not be capable of getting help if it is needed, so they depend on you for this step. If you are concerned about their safety or something else, don't be afraid to approach your pastor or a trusted friend for a referral to a counselor.

Don't embitter your children against their father. Your view of your husband will shape your children's view of their father. Attend to your feelings and needs. Avoid denial. But guard your tongue and your actions. Hatred poured over an open wound will not provide healing, but rather further festering.

Find support in other places. If dad isn't interested in being dad, look for help from others. Grandparents, uncles, friends, and the church community can step in to offer "skin on" help with the functions of fathering.

Introduce your children to their heavenly Father. God is the father of the fatherless. Psalm 68:5 tell us, "A father to the fatherless, a defender of widows, is God in his holy dwelling."

While he cannot replace their earthly father, God can and will provide authority and protection to meet many of their deepest father needs. Assist your children in understanding how God "fathers" them by giving them a unique identity, loving them unconditionally, and providing them with stability and protection. God will always meet their needs, even though they may not grow up with a father in the home.

You can find many descriptions and images of God's parenting role in the Bible, particularly in the Psalms. Read the Psalms to your children and pray the words with them as you read.

SEE "WHAT TO DO NEXT": WHEN A HUSBAND DOESN'T BELIEVE, PAGE 193.

Don't do motherhood alone. Isaiah 40:11 says, "He tends his flock like a shepherd: He gathers the lambs in his arms and carries them close to his heart; he gently leads those that have young." That's you, mom. God never intended for you to do motherhood alone. Rather, he longs for you to do motherhood in relationship with him. Let him carry you close to his heart as you mother. Let him lead you, because you are a mother and you have young.

SEE "WHAT TO DO NEXT": SUPPORT GROUPS FOR YOU, PAGE 163.

Make Room for Reflection

- *Check yourself.* Do you interfere unnecessarily when your husband does something differently than you? Do you tell him how to drive? Do you criticize his choices, like what he orders at a restaurant or what he wears on Saturday morning? Check how often you edit or interfere with the way he does something just because it is different from the way you do it.

- *Take the plunge.* Leave your husband alone with the kids so that he can figure it out on his own. Work through your hesitancies to leave by answering questions like, "Do I believe he can *learn* to handle what he might not yet have ever faced in fathering?" and "Do I trust his desire to help?"

- *Review your priorities.* Is it more important to have things done "your way," "the right way," or just "the way I like them done," or is it more important to share the load and let your husband grow? Time and again, moms report that they interfere with their husbands' fathering because it is "faster and easier" to do it themselves. Don't major on the minors and discourage dad by focusing on what really doesn't matter.

- *Keep a united front.* Do you decide ahead of time how you will handle disobedience, eating issues, sibling rivalry, and other subjects of childrearing and then stick together? You can always disagree out of sight and renegotiate when the kids aren't around.

- *Love him.* It might seem obvious, but it's easy to overlook. Take a moment to review your husband's best attributes. What attracted you to him at first? What motivates you to stay? When we invest our love in our husband, he rises to his best in his fathering (and in marriage too!)

Top Tips about Pops from MOPS

- I sent my husband and daughter out to eat donuts and go to the park while I painted a room by myself (even though I would have liked my husband's help).
- My husband is in the air force. He was deployed for one hundred days during our daughter's first birthday. He was trying to stay involved as a father, and her birthday present was a recording of songs and readings of her favorite books.
- He adores spending one-on-one time; he just doesn't like to be told that he needs to.
- I try to let my husband know either verbally or in a card or letter that I am proud of the father that he is, and that I know his children truly love their daddy.
- I show him that I can step back and let him father. I tend to go to a different room when our boys wrestle. Dad is there if someone bumps a head or gets a rug burn. I had to learn to back off from the time he took to be with his boys.

chapter ten

Let Dad Be Dad|

You run awkwardly in red, rubber ladybug boots,
With antennae flopping through blades of grass.
Trying to catch crickets, and tadpoles, and Daddy,
You push your pink sweat pants up above your knees,
> *as you splash the rain.*

I watch from the window, holding your infant brother to my breast
Thinking what a blessed life I live.
Pausing to feel all that is life, and to notice
> *The drop of mud clinging to your calf,*
> *The wind blowing your hair down into your eyes,*
> *The way you flick it out of your face,*
> *Then tuck it behind your ear with your little finger in a curl.*

I hear you call your father's name, "Daddy, wait."

He's loading wood into a rusty wheelbarrow for winter fires.
You're trying to get him to notice the wonder of a small
> *puddle of rain.*

I want to tap on the misty pane and yell,
But suddenly, God speaks first.
Daddy turns around and adds another roly poly to the
Floating leaf boat you've made.

I pause again to notice
> *The gentle glow in his face when he takes time for you,*
> *How high he holds you in the moistened air above his head,*
> > *offering thanks to the heavens in his own simple prayer.*
> *How he's careful not to let your little boots fall off.*

The patient way he wipes a raindrop from your cheek
before you wrap your hand around his finger and
pull him to the swing.

I am Mommy.
He is Daddy.
And all is right with my world.

—Julie Perkins Cantrell, "Daddy, Wait"

L et dad be dad" is a powerful concept built on several pivotal principles:

• Our children need fathers as well as mothers. Mothers and fathers are different and the differences are good.
• Men want to and can be good fathers.
• As moms, we can influence our children's father in powerful ways by making room for daddy.

Accomplishing this in the everyday of parental partnership is an ongoing process. As we've said, there are times when we need to step back, to resist the urge for control, to let go. In other moments, "letting dad be dad" means stepping forward to say what we do know. This give-and-take rhythm is characteristic of all healthy relationships. It is the mutual, interdependent expression of true partnership in parenting.

For example, imagine wallpapering a bedroom together for the first time. Neither of you has ever mastered such a skill. Both can read directions. Each can purchase supplies. Most likely one is better with color and texture while the other is better in the measurement category. Still, both abilities are necessary to complete the job. Through ebb and flow, together and separate, the shared task is accomplished.

How like parenting! At first, neither knows exactly how to diaper, feed, or discipline. Each brings differing natural insights. Both can learn and grow. Together in a mutual offering, the task of parenting is accomplished by both mom and dad.

There is something magnificent to be celebrated in dad's offering. As well, there is something to be invested in his parenting success. There are times to step back and let dad be dad, as we've underlined throughout the book. And there are some moments for stepping forward to share, to offer insight, to underline a strength, or to shape a weakness. We aren't saying you will know how to father better than your husband. If you think that, you've missed some of the messages in the last nine chapters! What we are saying is that *most* of the time moms can shape a father's fathering by stepping back. *Some of the time* we can influence by stepping forward. Knowing what to do when is the practice of letting dad be dad.

On-the-Job Training

One concept that will help you as you make room for daddy is this: you need to realize that your husband views fathering as a job. Huh? That's right, a job. What do we mean? Well, just as mothering is not something that naturally flows out of every woman, much of fathering must be learned. In the scheme of his life, a man views most of his activities as tasks to accomplish, functions to perform, things to complete. Life's tasks fit into boxes. He completes household chores that are written down. He prepares for work. He works. He husbands. He fathers. He relaxes. This makes sense to him.

There are two ways to view this mind-set. *First, it makes sense to him that his work is fathering*. Fathering expert Ken Canfield puts it this way, "Effective fathers don't really *subordinate* work priorities below family priorities; instead they *subsume* work priorities into the family priority. In other words, when they go to work they know *why* they are going there. It's not to put in their hours or make money or to make a name for themselves; they go to work in order to provide for their families and thus fulfill one of their fathering functions. These men are consciously 'being a dad' throughout the day, even while away from the home."[1]

Second, it makes sense to him that fathering is work. When presented to him in this way, suddenly fathering becomes something most men can immediately grasp and even enjoy. It moves from being something mysterious, vague, nurturing, and sensitive to the concrete world of task.

To him, bathing now becomes filling the bathtub with water, placing the baby in a bathseat, wetting, soaping, playing, rinsing, and toweling off. Feeding is strapping a child in a highchair, heating up the baby food, checking the temperature, tying on a bib, spooning food into the child's mouth, wiping hands and mouth, and setting the child free again. Diaper changing is removing an old diaper, discarding it in the trashcan, properly cleaning the wet bottom and applying the appropriate powder or ointment (ducking appropriately with a boy baby), and taping a clean diaper in place.

Moms can encourage on-the-job training in three specific areas of fathering: relational, personal, and spiritual fathering.

Relational Fathering

Over and over again, our surveys show that moms long for their husbands to "snuggle, hug, kiss, or verbally express how much they care for their children." To some men, relational fathering can be the most threatening aspect of fathering. One mom wrote us that her husband often feels that what he is doing with their son is "wrong"—like putting him down for a nap too early. She longed for him to have greater confidence in his own abilities as a father instead of looking to her.

What Dads Say About...

WAYS TO HELP HIM BOND WITH HIS CHILD
(FROM DADS IN OUR SURVEY)

- She showed me the proper way to feed him a bottle, and gives me an endless supply of confidence in my ability to be a good dad.

- She encourages me to spend time with my daughter, not only playtime but also feeding, bathing, and diaper changing. And she doesn't criticize the way I interact with my daughter, even if it's different than the way she interacts with her.

- She gives me books and articles on raising children.

- She gives me an opportunity to spend time with my child during the part of the day when my child is in a good mood.

- She says, "I think the baby is calling you," and she says that the baby responds to my voice more than she used to.

- I can't be a good father if I have someone looking over my shoulder and second-guessing everything I do. She is good at trusting me to make the right decisions.

- She sends the kids to me to answer even small questions that she could answer herself, just so the kids can communicate with me about issues that might be pretty insignificant but are good for our relationship.

Other ways to encourage dad to bond with the baby:

- Encourage him to look into the baby's eyes to make a connection with the baby.

- Give him a picture of the baby to carry around in his wallet—or put in his workplace.

- Have him help the baby discover several "firsts": her first touch of a snowflake; her first ride down a slide (on dad's lap); her first bike ride (in a safety seat with a helmet).

- Suggest he select a toy that becomes his toy to play with the child.

- Encourage him to find a favorite song that he plays or sings while he "dances" or moves around the room with the baby. Years from now, he can tell the child "that's our song."

Dads are helped by understanding that the forming and building of their relationship with their child is a task they can learn. Many moms testify that their husbands first "got this" when they were left alone with their child. One mom comments, "When I need to go somewhere by myself, I let him know that he is not baby-sitting the kids but is spending quality time with them (without me!). Sure, you can leave him lists and suggestions and instructions when you leave him, but leave! It's only when he is on his own that he'll have the chance to discover the gifts he has to offer in the life of his little one." When you're hanging around, it's tempting for him to let you lead him. When you're gone, he's free to figure it out for himself. He may object to such responsibility, feeling nervous that he'll be able to handle it. But offer reassurance—then go.

Dads we heard from deepened their relational skills through parent-child sports classes, father-child traditions like Saturday morning breakfasts out or Tuesday night Happy Meal nights, or even visiting school. All reported the vital ingredient here was spending time alone with the kids without mom in the picture.

One father tells of his nightly homecomings with poignancy. He'd enter to cheers of "Daddy's home!" and the "coin game" would begin. The coin game consisted of his grabbing whatever spare change was in his pocket and letting the kids climb and clamor over him, prying his fingers apart to obtain the money. This father was bemused that the game was over as soon as they pried his fingers apart until he realized that his kids really desired *him* more than the money. They looked forward to the predictability of the game and the physical connection with dad at the end of his workday.

The forming and building of the father-child relationship today creates the foundation for all dad-child interactions in the future.

SEE "WHAT TO DO NEXT": HOW TO HELP HIM USE "TOUCH LOVE," PAGE 171.

Personal Fathering

Each father will do fathering his own way. Mom's job? Step back and let him! He might dry his son's hiney off with a bib because it's the closest available object. He might take his kids fishing or flying or teach them to use the computer at age three because those are "his things." He might swell with pride at his three-year-old son's first piano performance even though it occurs in an elegant department store when mom is trying on clothes and he's supposed to be supervising the child. He might sit in the middle of the family room with his daughter, having a tea party and wearing the same colorful bracelets, rings, and bejeweled crown that she is wearing.

The point is, your husband will father in a way that is unique to his personality, and hopefully in a way that fits with his child's personality. "When it comes to fathering, there is a secret within each father that he longs to express with his kids, and it normally allows for some shared memories to develop between a father and child. . . . It is each man's individual expression of his fathering."[2] Our job as moms is to let dads discover their own style as dads and then get out of their way while they practice it.

Here are three ways we can accomplish this.

Free Him!

Some dads enjoy the baby years while others prefer the season when children have grown a bit and become more interactive. Some will be orderly in their care for their children— washing cups out after every use, restacking toys—while others are more "whatever" and get lost in the play of the moment. Some need a plan for everything from how they'll spend a simple Saturday afternoon to how they'll map out the family vacation. Others are more spontaneous, like the father in the watermelon picnic story at the opening of the book. Though the child remembered the dad as the "greatest dad ever," who was the other hero in that story? Surely as much credit for his success goes to the mother, who was willing to turn off the stove, skip dinner, and follow his lead. She stepped back and freed him to express his style. She encouraged rather than discouraged him.

Free your husband to father personally—in his own way.

Honor Him!

You may differ from your husband in his parenting style. In some ways you may not really even like what he does. But is his approach necessarily wrong? Probably not!

So honor him! What does that mean? "Honoring means watching your words—both *to* your husband and *about* him in front of your children."[3] In our words and our ways, we can magnify his investment in our children's lives by holding him up as valuable and special in their eyes.

Sometimes honoring means simply swallowing negativity or not giving into the temptation to be critical. He takes the kids to the park and brings them back, giving them an adventure and you an hour to yourself. When they arrive home, he takes off their shoes in the middle of the family room, only to spill sand and gravel everywhere. You have a choice: to criticize or to laugh and tell him that you have done the same thing. Either way, the mess has to be cleaned up, but your response will probably encourage or discourage his decision to try another such outing in the future.

In other moments, honoring means serving as his cheerleader. One mom writes, "Ever since my children were born, when dad comes home I say, "Daddy's home!" and we go to the door for hugs and kisses. I tell them often how much their daddy loves them." That's the idea. Honor your husband in his fathering efforts.

SEE "WHAT TO DO NEXT": THE BOTTOM LINE OF MARRIED LOVE, PAGE 185.

Appreciate Him!

Notice the unique contributions of your husband as a father and let him know you value those contributions and him because of them. Take advantage of the opportunity to use words to express your appreciation for his efforts.

Sometimes this can be hard because it is easy to overlook what he does in the midst of the daily chaos. When we asked moms what they appreciate about their husbands' fathering, they reported a variety of responses. This list may jump-start your ability to recognize what your husband does, so you can let him know that you appreciate his offering as a dad.

- I like the way my husband explains the whats and whys to our children—so I let him know that!
- We both have attended numerous classes on parenting. We actually attended seven classes before our son was born! I am usually the one who reads everything from magazine articles to books and I share this information with my husband. Then we talk, talk, talk! And I appreciate that.
- I tell him how much I love him and how much he means to us all.

When it comes to this very personal aspect of fathering, free him, honor him, and appreciate him—and watch dad be dad.

Spiritual Fathering

There is another vital dimension to fathering which often goes unnoticed in our world today. It's this: fathers influence the faith of their children. In fact, Sigmund Freud claimed that a child's psychological representation of his father is intimately connected to his understanding of God.[4]

Research shows this happens in several ways. First, while a mother can and does shape her child's more private relationship with a personal God, it is the father who helps that child put his or her faith in action in the community. One study revealed that mothers influence faith in personal matters but fathers impact their church attendance.[5] And further, without the involvement of fathers in the formation of a child's faith, Christianity is perceived as an "emotional, feminine experience."[6]

Second, when a father is involved in spiritual instruction alongside the mother, the experience is more likely to have a lasting impact on that child's life. Bottom line? The team approach of mom and dad together works best in every aspect of parenting, including the spiritual dimensions.[7]

This is probably not really big news to you. You may echo the thoughts of the mom who wrote, "I wish my husband had a stronger commitment to the Lord and a more complete understanding of his Word." Many moms who responded to our questionnaire agreed. In general, moms want dads to know how to equip their children in spiritual ways. They want them to take some spiritual role in the family.

In real life, most men find themselves held back by feelings of inadequacy. They look at the pastor and figure he can say more in a Sunday morning sermon than they could say in a whole year on the subject of God. Or that the youth workers and Sunday school teachers can talk freely about God. And there's you, the mom. Dad often sees you as the one who knows more about God. All this leads him to figure you'll handle the spiritual stuff.

But you still want him to be intentionally and deeply involved—right? If so, the following two simple tactics will make a difference.

Pray for Him

There's a great saying which goes, "Don't tell your husband about God; tell God about your husband." This means you must pray for him.

In her classic book *The Power of a Praying Wife,* Stormie Omartian charts the journey of her marriage from being a needling woman to becoming a woman who kneels. She cautions,

> the power of a praying wife is not a means of gaining control over your husband, so don't get your hopes up! In fact, it is quite the opposite. It's laying down all claim to power in and of yourself, and relying on God's power to transform you, your husband, your circumstances and your marriage. This power is not given to wield like a weapon in order to beat back an unruly beast. It's a gentle tool of restoration appropriated through the prayers of a wife who longs to *do* right more than *be* right, and to *give life* more than *get even.* It's a way to invite God's power into your husband's life for his greatest blessing, which is ultimately yours, too.[8]

Such a stance of prayer means relinquishment. As Nancy Swihart puts it, "Prayer releases us from the responsibility of having to know all the answers, having to be responsible for the actions or the neglect of our children's father. If we wish to be change agents in our husbands' lives, if we want to be catalysts for them to become better dads, then the only legitimate way is to join God's team."[9]

SEE "WHAT TO DO NEXT": PRAYING FOR YOUR KIDS' DAD, PAGE **194.**

Show Him Jesus

You join God's team by loving your husband with your faith. What does that mean? You let God's love flow through you to him. You love him for who he is and by encouraging him to become more of the person God created him to be. You show him Jesus with your hope, contentment, and joy.

In order to have faith and hope, we must realize that we are not in control of the whole wide world and all of its circumstances. Nor are we in control of the circumstances in our own little worlds; our own neighborhoods, homes, and families. God is. We are not in charge of changing people; God is. In his book *Beside Every Great Dad*, Ken Canfield writes,

> Instead of trying to change him, simply do what you believe God has called you to do in relation to him and his fathering. Your faithfulness is within your control—the results are not. Above all else, place your faith in the one who has declared himself "a father to the fatherless, a defender of widows" (Psalm 68:5), the one who is on record as saying he will "turn the hearts of the fathers to their children" (Malachi 4:6).[10]

SEE "WHAT TO DO NEXT": BECOMING A CHRISTIAN, PAGE **191**.

We're responsible only for loving other people the way God loves us. He knows us and loves us and forgives us for not being perfect, knowing that we are in process. And that's the way he wants us to love others. When we do, we are filled with an empowering sense of peace, contentment, and joy that spills out into our relationships with others all around us. It's this kind of love that lets dad be dad and lets your husband see Jesus in you!

Make Room for Reflection

- Look back over the various areas of fathering covered in this chapter (relational, personal, and spiritual). Which area is your husband's strongest offering right now? Which is his weakest? How can you underline his best offering—and support him in his weakest?

- Let him handle tasks in the way that seems best to him. Try making bedtime story time "daddy time." Or Saturday morning can be "pancake daddy time." Talk with your husband about a task he'd like to take on, help him with the details of how to do it, and then get out of his way!

- Check your heart—and your actions. On a scale of one to ten (one is great; ten, not so good) rate your ability to "free" your husband to father according to his personality. How can you move yourself closer to ten?

- What does "honoring your husband" mean to you? Make a list of "honoring" comments you might make to your husband. Once we think them up, we're more apt to say them. Next, take your "honoring" thoughts into the area of action. Tell him! Show him! Reward him!

Tops Tips about Pops from MOPS

- Anytime I leave the house, I think it encourages fathering.
- If my husband is working outside, I encourage him to take the children and let them help him. They take out their plastic hammers and work right alongside him.
- Our son is three and learning different things of life. One day he asked me a question regarding mortality. I wasn't quite

sure how to answer it, so I went and got my husband and all three of us talked about the subject as a family.

- Last night we had a family devotional, and he directed the time for us. He loved it, and so did the girls!
- We recently decided that my husband will take turns taking the kids out for breakfast on Saturdays to have some one-on-one time with the two older ones (seven and five).

Summing It Up

Mommy and Daddy Style

You have most likely come to the point where you want to make room for the daddy your husband can be in the life of your child. Let's review what we've covered:

- When a child is born, a father is born. Our role as moms is to understand daddy doubts, help him identify them, and love him through his adjustment to his days as a daddy.
- Fathers are important and yet they are struggling with a kind of daddy daze today. Our role as moms is to recognize the value of a daddy and to replace unrealistic expectations with realistic ones.
- The mother bond is a primary, foundational bond necessary for establishing all other bonds, the first one of which is the father bond. Our role as moms is to bond in order to launch.
- The longings of our hearts can distract us from the good we can do in influencing our husbands' fathering. Our job as moms is to identify what heart longing might be keeping us from launching our children.
- In an effort to be good moms, we can mishandle control, either assuming control for fathering functions or relinquishing our vital influence on our husbands' fathering. Our job as moms is to identify what mind warp might lead us to abuse our control.

- Moms have a choice to manipulate or to step back and allow dad to be a good dad, as well as a choice to be controlled or to contribute positive influence to our husbands' fathering. Our role as moms is to lay down the strings over our husbands' lives, to take up the strings of our own, and to move towards becoming partners in parenting.
- There's nothing wrong with a dad just because he parents differently than a mom. Our role as moms is to acknowledge and accept his difference as okay—even needed.
- Understanding original family issues helps strengthen mothering and fathering. Our role as moms is to do our homework on our original issues and to help dad do his as well.
- When dads parent differently, moms tend to interfere. Our role as moms is to recognize our tendency to interfere, and then move to inform instead.
- Fathering is something sacred to be celebrated and encouraged. Our role as moms is to get out of his way and let dad be dad.

Whew! We've covered a lot of territory, and this has become a long list of principles. But if you integrate even a few into your response to your husband's fathering, you will help shape his offering in the life of your child.

Remember this, mom: you have an enormous influence on your husband's success as a dad. You can either help or hurt his effectiveness in the life of his child. Make room for reflection. Browse through and use the resources in the next section of this book, "What to Do Next." Get going! Let your mommy style impact his daddy style by developing a mommy and daddy style together and watch your kids grow!

Here's how one version of mommy and daddy style looks after making room for daddy. In his own words, one dad tells how he received on-the-job training when his wife went out of town for a weekend conference.

I can't speak for all of us "XY" types, but I embarked on my journey with the mind-set that this time together without mom would give the kids and I chance to grow closer and spend some "quality time" together. I was correct in one respect—it was a journey.

My weekend started on Thursday, when I came home early from work to help my bride pack her bags and head out. She set us up well by making dinner, but left me to coordinate soccer practice and a school open house, both of which were happening at the same time (back and forth, back and forth).

With our oldest off to school on Friday, I made some progress—dishes, clothes, and kitchen floor. It was the only housework I would get done all weekend. During my caffeine-induced flurry I got a phone call. "Since you are doing the 'LuAnne-thing' this weekend, how about coming to McDonald's for lunch so the kids can play?" From there my plans took a turn toward the femininely social. After I got our kindergartener on the bus, we spent the next hour-and-a-half under the golden arches. Two cheeseburgers, two bags of fries, a drink, an apple pie, two kid cones, and a bee-sting later (neighbor's kid), I was rushing to a neighbor's house to drop off the kids so I could go to work for a meeting I "couldn't miss." Turns out I could have missed it. Needless to say dinner was the ever-nutritious frozen pizza, balanced out by glasses of milk.

Quiz time: If your daughter has a soccer game at 8:30 Saturday morning and you are the single dad of four kids ages 9 years to 17 months, how early do you have to wake up to make sure you are not late for the game? A: 7:30; B: 7:00; or C: 6:15. The answer is D: none of the above. It doesn't matter how early you start getting ready, someone is bound to use their breakfast to ruin their clothes or end up with a last-minute dirty diaper that you know you can't just shove into the car seat. Regardless, after the two soccer games, Saturday actually ended up being the highlight of our father-kid bonding. It was characterized by neighborhood hide-and-seek, a football game, a picnic lunch, and art projects. Of course, I also took the opportunity to mow the grass so I wouldn't die from estrogen poisoning. We closed out the day with me elbow-deep in suds during bathtime.

Mom came home Sunday morning and was waiting for us after church. She was tired and so were we, but it didn't seem to matter. Our family was whole again and life was good. It was good for her, and with that in mind, it was good for us. It forced me to realize that work isn't as important as it seems. It helped me to see the kids in a little different light; for the people they are and not "the kids" collective.

More important than all those things, LuAnne's weekend away underscored the truth that our family needs both mom and dad in order for it to function properly. In each of our strengths and in each of our weaknesses we form a single complete person who is doing our best to show our children what it means to work together the way God intended. I am very thankful for our family.[1]

What to Do Next

*N*ow that you understand the difference between and importance of both mommy and daddy styles, the following pages will help you know what to do next. Your life is busy; after all, you're a mom of young children. So you need to know where to look for what you need, and you need resources that get right to the point quickly.

Each part of this "how to" section offers practical advice to meet a specific need. The titles of each section are meant to help you quickly identify what you need. For a quick reference to the topics in this section, use the "Quick Topic Finder" on page 215.

So here it is, mom. We hope you'll find what you need in the following pages in order to help you make room for daddy—and continue to discover your own personal growth in the process.

How to Help You

Grumpy or Grateful: It's Up to You

> This may shock you, but I believe the single most signifi-
> cant decision I can make on a day-to-day basis is my choice of
> attitude.
>
> —Charles Swindoll

What is your attitude about your husband, especially as you consider his role as a father? Are you grateful for his efforts or grumpy about his shortfalls? Do you look for the good or nit-pick at the worst? Complain or compliment?

We have a choice of attitude each day, and that choice not only affects our general mood; it also affects the way we get along with everyone else around us, especially our husband. Our attitude is contagious, and it spills over into the lives of those around us, for good or not so good.

So for the next few days, why not take an attitude check and see where you land on the gratitude scale? Here are some ways to help you develop an attitude of gratitude.

Look at Yourself

A young mother was surprised when her husband told her that he felt like a failure as a father and husband. As they talked through his feelings, she realized she had spent much more time focusing on what was wrong with him instead of what was right. She realized she was too much of a perfectionist. She often forgot the mistakes she made, but almost always remembered the mistakes he made. She started her attitude adjustment by looking at herself. The day she began to change her attitude was the day she realized she needed to change her perspective.

Look for the Good

Get out a piece of paper and draw a circle that represents your relationship with your husband. Draw a slice to show what is not so good in the relationship. How big is it? Consider the rest of the pie. Is the way you speak to and about your husband proportional to what's good about him and your relationship?

Now identify the qualities you appreciate about him. Here are some words to trigger your thoughts:

Loving	Patient
Loyal	Humorous
Kind	Understanding
Encourager	Hard worker
Tolerant	Even-tempered
Creative	Willing to be flexible
Willing to share	Positive thinker
Intimate	Balanced
Organized	Responsible

Affirm the Good

Make a date and tell your husband all the things on your list that you appreciate about him. Try to catch him doing something that exemplifies these qualities and tell him that you are grateful for him. Recognize his improvement in other areas. Affirm him in front of others, especially your children. Affirm something you appreciate about him every day.

Be Realistic

Finally, you may have contributed to a tension in your relationship because of overly high expectations. To set things on a new course, you must make a conscious decision to do so. Use the following suggested prayer, or one like it, as a way of committing to be more of an encourager to your husband.

Lord, I confess that I have dwelt too much on what's not working right in my marriage and not enough on what is working right. I've attached strings to this relationship that were never meant to be. God, you didn't make your love and acceptance of me conditional, yet I have made my love and acceptance of my husband conditional. I do love my husband, but I confess that I have not shown him enough respect for the many wonderful qualities he does possess. I have not given him enough credit for the effort he puts forth and the improvements he has made. I ask you to forgive and cleanse me. By faith I now make a decision to turn things around, to express verbal appreciation, to forget more mistakes, to forgive my husband, and to remember more good things about him. I will make whatever adjustments are needed for him to know that I love, respect, and appreciate him. Empower me by your Spirit to keep my commitment. Amen.[1]

I thank my God every time I remember you.
—Philippians 1:3

Hidden Stuff in Your Heart

We take out the trash. We wash the dishes and clear off the kitchen counters. We even vacuum on occasion. We carefully attend to the condition of our homes in order to keep them off the "disaster area" list. But how much attention do we give to our hearts?

When the Bible says that the heart is to be guarded because it is the wellspring of life, it means that it is from our hearts that the rest of our attitudes get their cue. Depressed? Check the contentment quotient of your heart. Feel like griping? Once again, review your heart and you'll know why.

Rather than cleaning up the outer edges of our lives, we're wiser to pay attention to the deeper parts of ourselves. Running the vacuum cleaner through a few ventricles, we may discover a layer of dissatisfaction, envy, or even anger that we've stuffed out of sight.

There's no use trying to paste on a happy face or a good attitude to show in public if our hearts are cluttered with hidden issues. What's stuffed down in our hearts will sooner or later spill over into our days with our children, our neighbors, our coworkers, and God.[2]

Practicing Forgiveness

> Forgiveness is a simple sort of miracle. Forgiveness is a new beginning. Forgiveness is starting over and trying it again with the person who caused you pain. You start where you are, not where you wish you were, not where you would be if you could rearrange life.
>
> —Lewis B. Smedes

Forgiveness is the healing miracle needed in all loving relationships. It allows us to know and accept ourselves, and to know and accept others. There are two parts to forgiveness: receiving and giving. When it comes to encouraging our husbands to be the best dads they can be, we need to practice both receiving and giving forgiveness.

Receiving forgiveness means allowing yourself to be forgiven by God . . . for not being perfect, for desiring to be in control, for making mistakes. Receiving forgiveness means believing that God wants to wipe out all your guilt and love you for who you are.

Find a "God Spot" in your home, a comfy chair in the corner of the living room or bedroom, a sunny spot on the back patio or at the kitchen table, even on a pillow in a corner of a walk-in closet. Designate that special spot as a place you can go each day and simply be in order to receive God's love and forgiveness. Read 2 Chronicles 7:14, which tells us we must do four things in order to receive forgiveness: "If my people, who are called by my name, will humble themselves and pray and seek my face and turn from their wicked ways, then I will hear from heaven and will forgive their sin." First, we must humble ourselves and recognize that we are not perfect and we need God's forgiveness. Second, we must pray and ask God for forgiveness. First John 1:9 tells us that "if we confess our sins, he is faithful and just and will forgive us our sins." Third, we must "seek God's face" by reading the Bible and learning more about him. And finally, we must attempt to "turn from [our] wicked ways." We begin to live changed lives as we accept God's forgiveness.

Giving forgiveness to others comes more easily when we understand how we are forgiven. We forgive a husband for not being perfect. For sometimes falling short of our expectations. For not loving us or our children as well as we'd like. In forgiving, we release another from the responsibility to meet our needs. We practice forgiving even when the other person doesn't ask for or deserve it.

It's important to note that while we forgive, we don't always forget. Forgiving is remembering and still forgiving. As Richard Foster writes: "Forgiveness does not mean that we forget. That would do violence to our rational faculties. No, we remember, but in forgiving, we no longer use the memory against others."

Keep Growing

Mothering well doesn't require us to shelve our personal needs completely. Moms, too, have a legitimate need to grow as individuals, to develop their talents and abilities (doing), as well as to strengthen their character (being).

Today represents an important season in your life. You can't skip it or ignore it. And you can't ignore or neglect yourself in this season or you may find a gaping hole in the next. You probably have dreams and desires that need to be expressed. You may have creative juices that require an outlet of expression. The "you" that has been growing since your own birth doesn't cease to exist because you've given birth to another.

Here are some ways to grow yourself:

Sample Your Dreams

I'd like to. . .

- Play the piano.
- Raise golden retrievers.
- Be an Olympic medallist.
- Open a boutique.
- Start a cake decorating business at home.
- Design children's clothes.
- Write a book.
- Become a professional photographer.
- Be a clown at children's birthday parties.
- List your own possibilities:[3]

_____

_____

_____

_____

_____

Find a Nudger

A nudger is a person who encourages you to dream and then to act on your dreams. Do you have a nudger in your life?

- Identify three people who have served as nudgers in your past. How did they specifically nudge you?
- What qualities would you look for in a nudger?
- List three possible nudgers you might cultivate in your future.[4]

Grow Closer to God

- Read the Bible, even if you only have time to read one psalm a day.
- Find a church. Try the one in your neighborhood, or the one downtown.
- Recruit a prayer partner—on the phone, on the internet, on a neighborhood walk. Make time together to talk about your needs.
- Swap a book or article with your husband about something spiritual. Take fifteen minutes after the kids are in bed to share your thoughts with each other.
- Do something for someone else.

Battle of the Chores: Who Does What?

When we become parents, we enter a whole new level of responsibility with a whole new set of tasks. The fact is, most households run more smoothly and efficiently if those tasks are identified and delegated, so the responsible people understand who does what most of the time. And the delegation should not be based on gender stereotypes or assumptions passed down for generations. The delegating should be based on an understanding of "shared care" for the household and everything in it, including the children. When a father understands how much he is needed, he better understands the significance of his role. And children can help too!

Here are some ways to identify who does what:

1. Talk . . . about the Idea of Teamwork

- Discuss "gender stereotypes." How are you sharing those tasks differently or the same as your parents or his parents did? How do you want your family to be different in this way?
- Identify high-stress times of the day or week when "shared care" is most important. Determine quality standards or guidelines, but remember: when sharing the care of children or household, an important rule is to lower your expectations and be satisfied with results that may not be exactly the same as if you did it yourself.

2. Divide Tasks

- Write down a list of all routine, predictable tasks that need to be done, including childcare tasks.
- Sit down with your husband and discuss the tasks.
- Identify shared tasks.
- Ask him to choose his favorites.

- You do the same.
- Talk about the leftover tasks.

3. Make Children Part of the Team by Giving Them Age-Appropriate Tasks

Tasks for Two- and Three-Year-Olds

Load spoons into dishwasher
Help feed animals
Put away toys after play
Wipe table
Dry unbreakable dishes
Sweep (small broom)
Stir orange juice
Entertain infant
Bring in newspaper
Mop small area
Pour milk (small pitcher)
Empty wastebaskets
Dust furniture
Dig and pull weeds in garden
Fold dishtowels
Put away silverware
Load washer, unload dryer
Wipe mirrors (parent sprays)
Assist with stirring in cooking
Brush teeth, wash face
Tidy magazines, sofa pillows
Pick up trash in yard
Set table (from diagram)
Dress and undress

Tasks for Four- and Five-Year-Olds

Put away own clothes
Clean mirrors and glass alone
Set a complete table
Clean bathroom sinks
Help with simple desserts
Help load dishwasher
Take dirty clothes to hamper
Sort clean laundry
Hang towels after bath
Plant seeds
Grate cheese
Carry own dishes to sink
Mix salads
Put away groceries
Sort wash loads by color
Bring in the mail and put in proper place[5]

Support Groups for You

Support groups are not for the addicted or the bankrupt only. Support groups are for all sorts of people who come together to meet common needs. Mothers of young children especially benefit by forming or joining support groups, as this mom describes:

"I first came to MOPS (Mothers of Preschoolers) when a friend invited me. As I sat there with that group of women, I thought to myself, *How pathetic. I'm at a support group. Have I really sunk this low?* After I went through a complete session, I realized it was much more. It was fun and exciting to learn in all different areas and to help solve problems by sharing with other women."

Set up a baby-sitting co-op. Consider a food co-op to get discount prices on large quantities. Join a support group on parenting issues where you can gather with others struggling with the same questions and concerns.

Friends are a readily available source of help. They offer comfort, a sense of community, and practical assistance.[6]

For information about MOPS International, call 1-800-691-8061 or look up the web site at www.MOPS.org.

When You Need Help

Sometimes when moms cry out for help, the need is not physical but emotional, and sometimes that need can't be met by those around us. Sometimes you will feel helplessly overwhelmed and wonder if you need professional help. How will you know?

Most professionals agree that there are certain symptoms of psychological ill health:

- If you are in danger of hurting yourself or your children either verbally or physically, you need professional help.
- If you exhibit the symptoms of depression: loss of or increase in appetite, apathy, increased or decreased sleep, you may need professional help.
- If you think you are addicted to a drug or alcohol, you probably need professional help.

Areas of professional input can include self-development, marriage, sexual issues, childrearing issues, and physical issues.

To find a professional who can be of help, contact your local church, your insurance company, or your medical doctor. Friends are also a good source of referrals when your comfort level allows you to ask.[7]

How to Help Him

How to Help Him Bond before Birth

1. Find a fun way to announce the birth to your husband or family. (One mom wrapped up her early pregnancy test and gave it to her mother-in-law, saying it was an "early retirement gift." The mother-in-law couldn't figure out what it was, but when she did, she took the pregnancy test to show off at her retirement party!)

2. Invite your husband to attend one of your regular doctor visits, and make sure he comes for the ultrasound.

3. Spend time together each evening cuddling on the couch. Encourage dad to talk to the baby (tell him that the baby can hear, even in the womb) and stroke your tummy.

4. Rent the video or read the book *A Child Is Born* by Lennart Nilsson, which shows a baby's growth from conception to birth.

5. Track your baby's development in your womb by reading *What to Expect When You're Expecting* or by signing up for weekly bulletins from babycenter.com. Share the information with your husband.

6. Go shopping together for baby items that interest your husband, whether that be toys, car seat, stroller, crib, or clothes.

7. Take childbirth classes together.

8. Read out loud a devotional for expectant parents, such as *Expectant Moments* or *Miracle of Life*.

9. Have long discussions about names! Or, if you've chosen a name already, use it often when you talk about the baby.

How to Help Him Get Started as a Dad

These are suggestions written right to your husband about getting started in fathering. This is the page you can give him or use yourself in knowing what he needs.

1. *Get some practice.* Don't assume your wife magically knows more than you do. Whatever she knows about raising kids, she's learned by doing—just like anything else. And the way you're going to get better is by doing things too.

2. *Take charge.* Ultimately, if you don't start taking the initiative, you'll never be able to assume the childrearing responsibilities you want—and deserve. In all the times I've seen women pluck crying or smelly babies from their husbands' arms, I've never heard a man say, "No, honey, I can take care of this." So, if you find yourself in a situation like that, try a few lines such as: "I think I can handle things" or "That's okay; I really need the practice." And there's also nothing wrong with asking her for advice—you both have insights the other could benefit from. But have her tell you instead of doing it for you.

3. *Don't devalue the things you like doing with the kids.* Men and women have different ways of interacting with their children; both are extremely important to your child's development. So don't let anyone tell you that wrestling, playing "monster," or other so-called guy things are somehow not as important as the "girl things" your wife may do or want you to do.

4. *Get involved in the day-to-day decisions that affect your kids' lives.* This means making a special effort to share with your partner such responsibilities as meal planning, food and clothes shopping, cooking, taking the

kids to the library or bookstore, getting to know their friends' parents, and planning play dates. Not doing these things can give the impression that you don't think they're important or that you're not interested in being an active dad. And by doing them, you make it more likely that your wife will feel comfortable and confident in sharing the nurturing role with you.

5. *Keep communicating.* If you don't like the status quo, let your wife know. But be gentle. If at first she seems reluctant to share the role of child nurturer with you, don't take it too personally. Many women have been raised to believe that if they aren't the primary caregivers (even if they work outside the home as well), they've somehow failed as mothers.

6. *Get some support.* Even before your baby is born, you're likely to become aware of the vast number of support groups for new moms. It won't take you long to realize, however, that there are few, if any, groups for new fathers. Check out the support your wife finds through groups like MOPS and ask if there is an option for dads.[8]

How to Help Him Hear Your Advice

Does your husband get defensive when you share information or make suggestions about how to care for your children? If he does, you may assume that it's just plain easier to do it yourself, because you want to avoid the potential conflict. You give up rather than work to reach a better understanding and better partnership in your parenting. If you follow some of these tips about basic communication skills, he may hear your suggestions differently.

Pick the best time and place to share information. It's not so good to discuss parenting issues when the blood sugar is low and the stress level is high, like at the end of a long and exhausting day. Whenever possible, choose times when you both are relaxed and able to listen to each other.

Use "I" messages. Instead of saying "this is the way you should diaper the baby" or "you're not doing it right," say "When I diaper the baby this way, the diaper seems to stay fastened."

Avoid negative generalizations. Avoid "always" and "never." Saying "you *always* spoil their appetites before dinner" or "you *never* get them to bed on time" are negative generalizations bound to put him on the defensive.

Major on the majors. Share only the most important information or suggestions. Ask yourself, Will this make a positive difference for our children? Will this make a positive difference in his relationship with our children? Overlook the minor stuff.

Remember the compliments too. Criticism drives him away. Constructive suggestions are heard better when sprinkled with a few compliments. Tell him what he is doing well, even if his way is different from your way.

How to Help Him Connect with His Kids

William Pollack is an expert on boys and their fathers. Based on years of research and work with families, he offers these suggestions for successful father-child connection.

1. *Stay attached—no matter what.* It's amazing what the smallest gesture of love and connection can do. Even spending a short amount of time asking questions and connecting every day is better than giving up.

2. *Stand by mom.* Stay connected to your children and encourage them to stay connected to their mom. This teaches boys to respect women. Rather than teasing a boy about his need for his mother, encourage the relationship.

3. *Value who they are.* Instead of loving your children based on what they do, choose to value who they are. Love your child not for what you *wish* he had but for the qualities which come naturally to him.

4. *Develop your own style.* Develop your own style of playing, teaching, and nurturing your child. Research shows that your style, even though different from that of your spouse, is extremely valuable to your child.

5. *Do not be the "policeman" dad.* Try to avoid becoming the "heavy" or "bad cop"; instead, work with your spouse to provide discipline jointly and cooperatively.

6. *Show rather than tell.* Make the learning process one that teaches by "what I do" rather than "what I say."

7. *Be aware of your own "father longings."* Many men harbor memories about being teased or mistreated by their fathers for not being "masculine" enough or for disappointing their father. Muster the courage to go

beyond these memories and avoid repeating the same kind of shame-based upbringing for your own boys.

8. *Show emotions*. Let your children know that even as an adult, you sometimes feel lonely, vulnerable, or afraid, that you shed tears, and yearn for hugs. By expressing these things, you demonstrate that you can be trusted with all his feelings and experiences.[9]

How to Help Him Use "Touch Love"

Children need touch from dads. They need safe, strong, predictable, and dependable affection in their lives from a father who loves them. Resist the temptation to let mom hold the entire responsibility for meeting this need. Wear your baby in a backpack. If you use a bottle, take turns feeding. Let your toddler use your body as a human jungle gym. Read to your little ones on your lap. Play "Which Hand?" games.

Here are more touch tips for dads:

1. *Find your own personal touch style.* If you're ultra touchy, enjoy! Night-night hugs and tickle wars may flow from you as easily as a smile. If you're more reserved, a gentle hand squeeze can communicate love.

2. *It's never too late.* Whether your child is a preschooler or still an infant, you can still offer the benefits of touch. An older child might be surprised at the change so be patient and resist the urge to push.

3. *Be age-specific.* Infant massage can help you bond with your baby. Patty-cake is great for toddlers. Older kids appreciate a pat on the back or just an arm slung around their shoulder.

How to Help Him Find Friends

> I benefit greatly from networking with other moms and
> I'm not afraid to ask for insight from women I trust. This is a
> big help to me. I wish my husband had a similar group of dads
> that he could talk to. My friends also are great at following up
> and asking me how the situation is going, which shows they
> care, but it also makes me feel accountable. This is another
> area my husband could use help in.
>
> —A mom

How can you help your husband find the kind of friends
who offer advice, normalize his parenting challenges, and
encourage him in the midst of fathering? Or the kind of
friends who will do things as dads together with kids? Choose
either a one-on-one mentoring relationship, or encourage
him to organize a small group.

Where to Look
Check with your church. Some have parenting classes or
    fellowship groups or a list of mentors.
Community support groups, especially those centered on
    parenting or fathering classes.
Neighborhood groups or school groups.

Meeting Guidelines
Commit to meeting regularly.
Center on healthy parenting.
Establish a safe environment for sharing.

Friendship Qualities
In their book *Safe People,* Drs. Henry Cloud and John
Townsend recommend these qualities to look for in safe
friendships that will promote personal growth:

Acceptance and grace

Mutual struggles, although they do not have to be the same struggles

Loving confrontation

Both parties need other support systems as well

Familiarity with the growth process where both parties have "entered in" and have some knowledge of the process so as to avoid the blind leading the blind

Mutual interest and chemistry, a genuine liking

An absence of "one-up and one-down" dynamics

Both parties in relationship with God

Honesty and reality instead of overspiritualizing

An absence of controlling behavior[10]

How to Help Him Understand Child Development

Mental Development

Jean Piaget theorized that all children progress through four basic periods along the path of mental development.

Stage	Development
Sensorimotor (Birth to 2 years)	The child encounters his world in terms of action. There is a lack of object permanence: when someone is out of sight, in the child's mind he has disappeared and no longer exists. (No wonder a child hollers when mom and dad leave for a night out!) As the child learns to control his own body during the first two years of his life, he acquires the ability to mentally represent objects that are no longer present physically.
Preoperational (2–7 years)	The child encounters his world in terms of thoughts. With the emergence of language, the child continues to represent his world mentally. But his thinking is dominated by his own perspective. (When a six-year-old says she is right, there is no persuading otherwise.)
Concrete Operational (7–11 years)	The child encounters the world in terms of relations. Logical thinking is applied to solve concrete problems. (Science fairs with fifth-graders are a scene where proof must be demonstrated!)
Formal Operations (11 years and up)	The child encounters the world in terms of theories. At last, he is capable of abstract, complex, mature thought. (Ah . . . the joys of dissecting the great truths of life—and being understood.)

Social Development

Erik Erikson suggested that psychological development is the result of an interaction between our biological needs and the social forces we encounter in everyday life. Development proceeds through eight stages. In each stage, we are confronted with a basic crisis that can be resolved in one of two ways.

Stage	Crisis
Stage 1 (Birth to 1 year)	**Trust vs. Mistrust** Can I trust the world? If mom leaves, will she return? If I cry, will my needs be met?
Stage 2 (2–3 years)	**Autonomy vs. Shame and Doubt** Can I control my own behavior? Can I learn to obey? Can I stop the fit, keep the bed dry, eat my peas?
Stage 3 (4–5 years)	**Initiative vs. Guilt** Can I explore my limits and become independent of my parents? Will dad answer me if I ask "why" again?
Stage 4 (6–11 years)	**Industry vs. Inferiority** Can I master the necessary skills to adapt? Will I be able to learn to read? Will math begin to make sense? Will it be okay to ask questions when it doesn't?
Stage 5 (12–18 years)	**Identity vs. Role Confusion** Who am I? What do I think about issues like suicide, drugs, abortion, pollution? What does it mean to know Christ?
Stage 6 (young adulthood)	**Intimacy vs. Isolation** Can I give myself fully to another? Will I be able to trust another with my deepest self? When the going gets tough, will I choose to stay?
Stage 7 (adulthood)	**Generativity vs. Stagnation** What can I offer succeeding generations? Will my life make a difference? Is my work worth the effort?
Stage 8 (maturity)	**Integrity vs. Despair** Have I found contentment and satisfaction through my life's work and play? Will God greet me with, "Well done, my good and faithful servant?"

Moral Development

Lawrence Kohlberg found evidence to suggest that morality (ideas or rules that govern human conduct) develops in stages. Individuals usually progress from one stage to the next, though few actually arrive at the most sophisticated level of morality.

Level One:	**Premoral**—Birth to 7 years
Step 1	Good equals what is pleasant. Bad equals what is painful. Rules are obeyed in order to avoid painful punishment.
	"Okay! I'll share my toys! Just don't spank!"
Step 2	Right and wrong are judged on the basis of what pleases (and usually pleases the self). Rules are obeyed to obtain rewards and have favors returned.
	"If I share my treats, will you shares yours?"
Level Two:	**Conventional**—7–15 years
Step 1	Good boy/girl morality. Considerations of others enters the picture with high importance placed on the approval of others. Rules are obeyed to obtain approval.
	"If I let you borrow my ribbon, will you like me?"
Step 2	Emphasis on law and order. Right and wrong judged by obeying the laws and authority. Rules are obeyed in order to avoid censure by authorities.
	"The Bible talks about giving one-tenth of our income. I'd better give $10 out of this $100 I just received."
Level Three:	**Principled Morality**—15 years and up
Step 1	Accepted law. Individual rights are important as they relate to the majority. Rules are obeyed to maintain community welfare.
	"Our government ought to do something to make sure the homeless folks have homes. I pay my taxes!"
Step 2	Morality of individual's own conscience. Universal principles like the Golden Rule adopted. Rules obeyed to avoid self-condemnation.
	"I need a new coat. But so does that old guy out there on the street. Maybe I'll give him mine."[11]

How to Help Your Marriage
The ABCs of Love

> Hatred stirs up strife, but love covers all transgression.
> —Proverbs 10:12 (NRSV)

"I accept you as you are."

"I believe you are valuable."

"I care when you hurt."

"I desire only what is best for you."

"I erase all offenses."

We could call that the ABCs of love. And I don't know of anybody who would turn his back on such magnetic, encouraging statements.

There is nothing shallow about authentic love. Nor is it a magic wand we whip out and wave over a problem with a whoosh, hoping all the pain will go away. Real love has staying power. Authentic love is tough love. It refuses to look for ways to run away. It always opts for working through. It doesn't cop out because the sea gets stormy and rough. It's fibrous and resilient. . . .While the world around us gives the opposite counsel, love stands firm.[12]

Can You Change Your Husband?

> An excellent wife, who can find? . . . Her husband . . . praises
> her.
>
> —Proverbs 31:10, 28 (NASB)

A wife is not responsible for her husband's life. She is
responsible for her life. You cannot make your husband something he is not. Only God can do that.

I think it was the evangelist's wife, Ruth Graham, who
once said, "It is my job to love Billy. It is God's job to make
him good." I'd call that a wonderful philosophy for any wife
to embrace.

Wife, it's your job to love your husband. It's God's job
to change his life.

And wives who are truly obedient to Christ will find that
he will honor their secure spirit.[13]

Growing Your Marriage

You've probably heard the saying: "The best thing I can do for my children is to love their father."

The healthy growth of your marriage helps your husband be a good father. In a healthy, growing marriage, you communicate well. You partner well. You encourage each other to be all God created you each to be. You take care of each other's hearts and listen to each other's thoughts and feelings and needs.

How do you continue to grow your marriage?

Here are fifteen tips gathered from married people, excerpted from a column by Sharon Randall:

1. Always listen to each other. When you are wrong, say you are sorry; when you are right, shut up.
2. Don't tie the knot in a halfhitch; plan to stay married forever.
3. Never go to bed angry; talk until you get over it or get so tired you forget why you were mad.
4. Laugh together. If you can laugh at yourself, it won't be hard.
5. Never embarrass or criticize or correct one another in public; and try not to do it in private either.
6. Remember that we're all the least lovable when we need love most.
7. Beware, both in marriage and life, of the myth of perfectionism; it exists only as a lie.
8. On the days when you don't like each other, remember that you love each other; pray for the "good days" to come again and they will.
9. Tell the truth, only the truth, and always with great kindness.

10. Kiss for at least ten seconds every day without fail; do it all at once or spread it out.

11. Examine your relationship at intervals; feel it, question it, know its vulnerabilities; keep it moving in the direction you both want.

12. Be content with what you have materially, honest about where you are emotionally, and never stop growing spiritually.

13. Remember that to love someone is to wish them the best. Always wish each other the best.

14. Never yell unless the house is on fire; whisper when you argue.

15. Be friends, as well as lovers; in a blackout, share the flashlight; then make electricity together.[14]

The Legacy of Love

A mother recently asked how to keep love alive in her marriage, amidst the challenge of raising young children. "I often feel totally dry and empty as if I have nothing left to give my husband," she says.

The driest emotional times in any marriage are often during those days of raising young children. Intimacy seems almost an obligation rather than a joy. Author (and funny lady!) Liz Curtis Higgs remembers being a nursing mother and warning her husband not to touch her. "This body can do only one thing at a time," she told him.

Maintaining a sense of intimacy is difficult in the midst of crying children and 2 A.M. feedings. We meet our children's needs first because they are more demanding. But we heed the words of an older mom who wishes she had done it differently. "I woke up one morning after the kids were grown, and realized that I no longer knew the man I married," she said. "Through the years, we had drifted apart emotionally."

The marriage relationship is supposed to be the primary relationship in the family because children will come and go. But keeping love alive takes an intentional effort during the distracting times of raising children. Try to plan regular mini-getaways while your children are young. If you can't get a whole night away together, try what one couple did. They hired a baby-sitter for the evening, got a hotel room, had a romantic picnic dinner in the room (you could order room service), returned home before midnight, and brought their kids back to the hotel in the morning for breakfast and a swim in the pool before checking out of the room.

Another way to weave intimacy into your family life and keep love alive is to tell your love story to your children. Talk about how you met each other and describe the day and way you got engaged. Not only will that pass on a message to your children, it will remind you of the reasons you married each other in the first place.

On your anniversary each year, get out your wedding pictures and show them to your children. Leave the photo album on the coffee table for a few days. Also, when you attend another wedding with your husband, listen carefully to the vows and recommit yourself to those promises. Get remarried, again and again.

Keep love alive by investing your time and energy and attention in each other. The return on the investment grows steadily through the years.

Babies and Budgets: Working Together as Parents

Parents quickly learn that a "bundle of joy" can cost a bundle of money and the adjustments to those expenses can cause a bundle of tension in a marriage. Although estimates vary, the U.S. Department of Agriculture claims that most families spend between $6,000 and $12,000 a year for a child, depending upon their income. Raising a child from birth to age eighteen can run more than $200,000. That's enough to give any parent a "yikes" attack! No wonder finances and budget woes can cause problems in a marriage with children.

Many problems come from differences in backgrounds and training, priorities and expectations about money, which are magnified when couples become parents. Here are some tips to help you think together about your expectations and realities in the area of finances.

1. *Communicate: decide to talk about money.* This sounds simple, but many couples don't like to talk about finances. Just do it. Discuss your attitudes about spending and saving. What does the word *budget* mean to you? In your family growing up, who paid the bills? What are your priorities when it comes to how you spend your money?

2. *Create a budget.* A budget makes your life easier, but you have to agree that a budget is necessary. Who will do what in the process? Will you commit to working together on the task? Will you be realistic about how much money you have and how much money you spend?

3. *Determine your annual income.* That means writing down how much money comes in from every source in a year's time, including salary, bonuses, gifts, and tax refunds. That total, divided by twelve, becomes a monthly budget.

4. *Determine your monthly expenses.* Write down everything you actually spend in a two-month period. Try to divide expenses into categories: housing, food, clothing, automobile, insurance. No doubt, everything costs more than you thought, and the costs get bigger as the children grow up. How do your monthly expenses match your monthly budget?

5. *Create a plan for the future.* The simplest plan is to spend less than you have and save the rest.

6. *Communicate some more.* Talk about the plan. Share the responsibility of doing the bills and keeping the records for the family finances. Though one of you is bound to be better in this area, both of you should be familiar with the finances.

The Bottom Line of Married Love

One day we will each stand before Jesus and give an account of how well we loved our friends, our family, our children, people we don't even know, and our husband or wife.

As you picture yourself giving an account of your support of your spouse, consider:

To love is to respect.
To love is to honor.
To love is to offer tender affection.
To love is to choose commitment—over and over and over and over again.
To love is to show kindness and mercy.
To love is to forgive.
To love is to invest.
Love is expressed in word, action, belief, and participation.

As you love your spouse, consider standing before Jesus and giving an account as to how you invested in each other's gifts for the kingdom of Jesus.

How can you offer the pillar support of your love?
How will you move aside, allowing for growth?
How might you take on tasks, freeing another for service?
How can you mirror giftedness of another, clarifying an offering?[15]

How to Help Grow Your Faith

Wisdom for Moms

In days (and nights) when we feel like we're literally *feeling* our way through motherhood, we hunger for life. What we specifically seek is the wisdom to know how to do this job. *Am I moving in the right direction? Will my investment today pay off tomorrow? Will my child grow up to be healthy and whole?* we wonder. And we want wisdom. Oh, how we want it.

The Hebrew word for wisdom is interesting. You would think it meant something like "smart," even "genius." Nope. It literally means "skill for living." Someone who is wise is "skilled for living life well." Hmmm. That's more than "smart." Wisdom is what we want.

So how do you get wisdom? Hmmm again. Perhaps by recognizing where you don't have it, where you're not skilled. We make mistakes. We think we know our kids. We analyze their patterns and make conclusions about their needs and then, suddenly, they surprise us. They send us reeling by moving in a direction we never expected. We believe we've made a right choice. Later, life turns upside down on the very "right-looking" choice we previously made. Being skilled for living wise means facing what we don't know.

Then, being wise also means recognizing there is Someone who does know, and reaching out to him. Sure, this can be awkward, vulnerable, humbling, and even scary at first. But for those of us who want to live life well—skillfully—it's wise to take advantage of a heavenly offer of assistance.

We may not be skilled for living life all the time, but God is. He offers truth as well as hints for how to use it in life. God offers words of life for moms. It's called wisdom. He's a wise guy.[16]

What Is a Real Christian?

How can you know if you're really a Christian?

To begin with, a real Christian knows God. But knowing God is different from knowing about him. Imagine trying to choose a spouse just by reading about him or her. You might have a lot of information, but you probably wouldn't feel ready to make a decision until you'd met her in a personal encounter. Until then, you couldn't honestly say you knew that person. It's the same with God.

God created us for relationship with him. However, sin (wrong moral choices) entered the world through the first man and woman when Adam and Eve chose to disobey God (Genesis 3). Because God is without sin and can't tolerate evil, Adam and Eve's sin separated them from God. Every individual who has lived since has followed in their footsteps. The Bible says, "All have sinned and fall short of the glory of God" (Romans 3:23). It also says that "the wages of sin is death" (Romans 6:23). If there were no sin, there would be no death. But everyone has sinned, so everyone must die. It's a pretty bleak picture.

Fortunately, God has an answer. His answer is Jesus Christ, God in human form. The Bible teaches that Jesus came and lived a perfect life on earth so he could take the punishment for our sins on himself. He died on the cross for our sins and came back to life, never to die again. The authenticity of all religions, groups, or individuals that claim to be Christian can be tested by whether their beliefs about Jesus Christ line up with the teaching of the Bible.

What Does a Christian Look Like?

A real Christian knows God because his Spirit lives in her. Sound spooky? Amazing, but true! Because Christians have the Spirit of God, they display godly attributes. These include purity, love, and obedience.

187

God is holy and without fault. His Holy Spirit living in his people gives them the desire and ability to live pure and holy lives. This involves both doing good things and refraining from bad things. If an individual's life is characterized by greed, depravity, and dishonesty, she is probably not a Christian. The apostle John wrote, "Anyone who does not do what is right is not a child of God" (1 John 3:10).

God is love (1 John 4:8), so someone who has his Spirit in him is going to love God as well as other people. This requires a word of explanation. In North American culture, love has come to be equated with warm feelings that are more or less beyond our control. If they are absent from a relationship, we conclude we don't love that individual. But God's love means desiring and acting on what is best for another individual, regardless of how we feel. Love for others prompts us to reach out to and help meet the needs of those around us—even those who may annoy or oppose us. In 1 John 3:18 we read, "Dear children, let us not love with words or tongue but with actions and in truth."

Love for God prompts us to seek to know him better. One avenue for knowing him is prayer and Bible study. If we love someone, we will want both to talk to him and hear from him. One of God's primary means of speaking to us is through the Bible. And in prayer, we both talk and listen to him. Another way to know God better is through involvement in a church, where we can worship him and grow in our understanding of his Word, the Bible.

In addition, an individual with the Spirit of God inside him will obey God. The apostle John wrote, "We know that we have come to know him if we obey his commands" (1 John 2:3). Jesus Christ is Lord and master in a Christian's life, not because he is a tyrant, but because he made us, gave his life for us, and always does what is best for us. He deserves first place. Recognizing this is an act of worship. Worship can be expressed in words of praise, but also in action, when a Christian lives in a way that acknowledges God's rightful authority in his life.

Growing as a Christian

The following pursuits will help you grow in your relationship with God for the rest of your life.

Read the Bible regularly. The Bible is the written record God has preserved for the express purpose of revealing himself to us. As you read, you will not only gain a better intellectual understanding of God's ways. He will also begin to change your thoughts and actions. Paul instructed the Romans to "be transformed by the renewing of your mind. Then you will be able to test and approve what God's will is—his good, pleasing and perfect will" (Romans 12:2). Reading Scripture is a great way to renew our minds. When we saturate ourselves with God's Word, our thoughts will gradually begin to follow the pattern of God's ways, rather than the pattern of the world.

While reading, look for examples to follow and instructions to obey. Start by reading the words of Scripture in the Bible. What is *God* saying to you through his Word?

Meet with other Christians. Find a church that believes the Bible, honors Christ, and is interested in helping you grow as a Christian. Through the church you will gain valuable instruction from and insights into God's Word. But just as importantly, the individuals in your church are your new family. Spend time with them. They are the people who will love you, encourage you, support you, and keep you on the right path when you start off in the wrong direction. And as God's Spirit works in you, you will find opportunities to do the same for them. In Hebrews 10:25 we read, "Let us not give up meeting together, as some are in the habit of doing, but let us encourage one another." God created us for community. He didn't intend for us to go it alone.

Begin to pray. Communication is the key to any relationship, and it's the same with God. You can talk to him about *everything.* Tell him your doubts, fears, struggles, temptations, joys, triumphs, sorrows. He can handle it all. Ask him for what you need—and ask him to *show* you what you need (it may not always be what you think)! Thank God for all the wonderful things he has done for you. Start paying attention to God's blessings throughout the day and remember to thank him for them. Set aside a specific daily time to pray, but try to listen and talk to God as you go about your activities as well.

Some other suggestions:

- Ask God to reveal himself to you if you still have doubts about him.
- Spend time enjoying creation.
- Don't hesitate to ask questions. Write them down and take them to a mature Christian.
- Talk to people who've been Christians for a long time about their experiences with God.
- Read Christian authors. Ask your Christian friends for a list of suggestions.
- Remember that questions and moments of doubt are normal and legitimate. Talk to God and your Christian friends when you struggle with doubt and discouragement.
- Keep a journal of your thoughts and feelings, as well as the lessons God teaches you through Scripture.
- Set a daily time to pray and read the Bible. Act on it.[17]

Becoming a Christian

To understand a person's need for God, look first at your own need for hope and where you've been seeking it. Your children can't provide you with the consistent hope you need; they have too many needs themselves. And what about your spouse? Can he fill your need for hope? The truth is, we are married to people who are in process. No human, however intimately attached we may be to them, can meet our deepest need for hope because no human can love perfectly.

Only God can fill the longings of your heart, because only God loves you perfectly. Only he can provide the eternal source of stability from which to hang your marriage.

But a deeper understanding of our need for God comes when we turn the issue around. Instead of looking at the ways we attempt to *get* hope, let's look at our ability to *provide* hope to others in our lives.

When your children approach you with needs day in and day out, you can't always deliver. There's simply not enough of you to meet each request for another glass of juice, a listening ear, a comforting hug. Sometimes you can't be there. Sometimes you're just too tired and distracted and running on empty yourself. You reach into your reservoirs of wisdom and patience and realize you have none left to meet your children's needs or solve their problems.

The same is true in your relationship with your spouse. You aren't always loving, always kind, always forgiving, always *for* him. In fact, sometimes you're selfish. Sometimes you're rude. Sometimes you're downright stubborn and insist on your own way.

So where is hope when you fail?

Here's lasting hope. Eventually you realize that you can't find the hope you need in your children or your mate. Neither can you be their hope.

There's a simple reason why this is the case. It's called *sin*. Sin is part of our human nature; we are imperfect people living in an imperfect world. We can't do it right by ourselves. Because God is perfect and can't be in the presence of imperfection, our sin separates us from him—from the very Source that can provide hope for us.

God news! God loves you and wants to be in relationship with you. So he chose to take care of this sin problem himself by allowing his Son, Jesus, to die on the cross. His death pays for your sins and makes it possible for you to be forgiven for all the imperfect blotches in your life. All you have to do is ask. When you grasp the truth that you can't always deliver or receive the hope needed when you *look down* at your children or *look over* at your spouse, you are ready to *look up*.

When you reach the end of yourself and your ability to be everything for those around you, you turn to God and receive his hope with this simple prayer: *Dear Jesus, I need hope. When I look down, all I see is the responsibility of my children. They can't provide what I need. I can't provide all they need. When I look over, I see the needs of my mate. I can't find all that I need there. I can't always love him or her the way I want to. Their love is imperfect, and so is mine. I believe that you died on the cross for my sins and imperfections. Please come into my life as my Savior. I attach myself to you as the Source of my life. I hang my life on you and on no other. Please come into my life and begin a relationship with me. Amen.*

If you prayed that prayer just now as you read it, you can be sure that today you have a new reason to hope! You may not feel so different immediately, but you can start living with the promise that Jesus loves you and that he will help you on a day-to-day basis. You no longer have to wonder where you'll find your hope and strength. In fact, your marriage was designed to be lived in partnership with your mate, with Jesus as your Leader.[18]

When a Husband Doesn't Believe

In his book *Unbelieving Husbands and the Wives Who Love Them,* Michael Fanstone offers advice for those listening who long to share their faith with their spouse. Listen in:

Expect to be happy. Don't expect to be miserable and have insurmountable problems because your spouse is not a believer.

Expect your spouse to be unreasonable. Sin is not an issue, and your godliness may be threatening, convicting, and confusing.

Expect problems as a part of your life. You may have a tendency to idealize Christian marriages and blame many normal problems on the fact that your spouse is not a believer. The truth is, many problems you face are common to all marriages and are not solely due to the fact that your spouse is not a Christian.

Look for positives. What qualities attracted you to each other in the first place? In what ways is your spouse growing? What are some of the things your spouse does that please you?

Be genuine. Act out your faith with sincerity and conviction.

Be loyal. Don't advertise that your spouse is not a believer.

Put God first. In all things, Christians are commanded to put God first, but ask yourself, can you please your spouse without detracting from God?

Rely on the character of God.[19]

Praying for Your Kids' Dad

There are times when we feel at a loss to influence our husbands' fathering. In such moments, we turn to the power of prayer. The hope and power of prayer are available not just in the pinches of life but also in the everyday, if we take advantage of it.

In her best-selling book *The Power of a Praying Wife*, Stormie Omartian writes, "Have you ever had someone pray for you when you couldn't think straight, and after they prayed you had complete clarity and vision? I believe this is what can happen for our husbands when we pray about their parenting."[20]

Try offering up a simple prayer for the father of your children. Include items such as his patience, his confidence, his insight into their needs, his discipline and interaction with them. Consider their needs through various developmental seasons, and his comfort level with each stage and age. Pray through his strengths and weaknesses and for his own personality to be freed to father.

You might incorporate a prepared prayer like the one Stormie offers in her book:

Lord, teach _____ to be a good father. Where it was not modeled to him according to Your ways, heal those areas and help him to forgive his dad. Give him revelation of You and a hunger in his heart to really know You as his heavenly Father. Draw him close to spend time in Your presence so he can become more like You, and fully understand Your Father's heart of compassion and love toward him. Grow that same heart in him for his children. Help him to balance mercy, judgment, and instruction the way You do. Though You require obedience, You are quick to acknowledge a repentant heart. Make him that way, too. Show him when to discipline and how. Help him to see that he who loves his child disciplines him promptly (Proverbs

13:24). May he never provoke his "children to wrath, but bring them up in the training and admonition of the Lord" (Ephesians 6:4). I pray we will be united in the rules we set for our children and be in full agreement as to how they are raised. I pray that there will be no strife or argument over how to handle them and the issues that surround their lives.

Give him skills of communication with his children. I pray he will not be stern, hard, cruel, cold, abusive, noncommunicative, passive, critical, weak, uninterested, neglectful, undependable, or uninvolved. Help him instead to be kind, loving, soft-hearted, warm, interested, affirming, affectionate, involved, strong, consistent, dependable, verbally communicative, understanding, patient. May he require and inspire his children to honor him as their father so that their lives will be long and blessed.

Lord, I know we pass a spiritual inheritance to our children. Let the heritage he passes on be one rich in the fullness of Your Holy Spirit. Enable him to model clearly a walk of submission to Your laws. May he delight in his children and long to grow them up Your way. Being a good father is something he wants very much. I pray that You would give him the desire of his heart.[21]

How to Help When You're Not Married to the Father of Your Children

When the father of your children doesn't live in your home, your challenges are different and more difficult. Still, there is much you can do to foster the "fathering component" for your children. Here are some suggestions.

1. Seek help and support for yourself first. You need to find help in healing your feelings first. You need a safe place to express your emotions, a place other than your children. Seek out help from others who can empathize with you—friends, support groups, other single moms, and, if possible, get counseling to sort through your emotions. Don't wait for others to approach you and offer help; assess your own needs and ask others for specific help, such as for baby-sitting, financial advice, and help around the house.

2. Seek spiritual support. A church is a good place to start, but you may have to change churches to find the support you need if you no longer feel like you and your children "fit" in the church community you've been part of. The truth is, some churches meet the needs of single moms and their children better than others. Also, seek God's comfort in prayer and in the Bible. True healing can come through knowing God. He may not miraculously change your circumstances or your pain, but he promises to be with you and give you strength to persevere. Pray that God will be your children's father and draw them to himself. Also pray for your children's father, for his spiritual journey and for his involvement in parenting your children.

3. Seek help and support for your children. Be sure your children have a safe place to express their feelings. Again, you may need to change some of your circles of friends in order for your children to feel supported. Find a church with a good youth program. Encourage friendships with children who are supportive.

4. *Maintain healthy communication with your children.* One of the challenges is to consider their needs while still taking care of yourself. Your children need to work through their emotions about what has happened, so you need to ask them about their feelings and keep the lines of communication open. The goal is to find a positive process for coping with conflict and changes. Counseling may be helpful if your child shows signs of anger, withdrawal, or depression.

5. *Find healthy role models for your children.* Your children have important needs that can best be met by men, and they will benefit from a masculine perspective they cannot get from you. They need to see someone regularly who models healthy, Christian male behavior. If your children's father is not in a place to provide this, seek men who can and will. The pool of possibilities may include extended family members, a Sunday school teacher, children's or youth pastor, youth leaders, school teacher, coach, or neighbor. Once discovered, pray for the individual, encourage him, and accept his uniquely male way of interacting with your children.

6. *Present a healthy home atmosphere.* Give your children as much security as possible by maintaining regular, predictable schedules. If your children are going back and forth between your house and their father's house, try to maintain similar schedules and rules about homework and bedtimes, etc. As soon as you are able, connect yourselves with at least one other emotionally healthy family so that your children are exposed to a household where the husband and wife show love for each other and work together to build confident children.

7. *Adopt a positive attitude toward your children's father.* The last may be the most difficult, but probably results in the greatest benefit for your children. Unless you have strong reasons to suspect physical or emotional abuse, a civil relationship between you and their father will give your children a

needed sense of security. As you encourage him to be their father, you might view the interactions as you would an objective business relationship. Above all, beware of the four most common hindrances to this process:

- *Avoid bad-mouthing the other parent.* Known today as the Parent Alienation Syndrome, this behavior seeks to alienate the child from the other parent, and is even getting legal attention in some states.
- *Don't expect your child to be a messenger between mother and father.* Don't expect them to carry messages such as "You tell your father that I won't do that." Adult communication should be handled at the adult level, from adult to adult, not through the child.
- *Don't let your child get caught in the middle of your financial issues.* For instance, when your child needs eight dollars for the school pictures, don't put him in the middle of a disagreement, such as "I'm not paying that eight dollars. You get it from your father!"[22]
- *Don't expect your child to play "I spy" for you.* Don't ask your child, "What did your father do yesterday?" or "What did your dad buy this week?" or "Who is your dad spending time with?"

How to Help by Reading On . . .

Marriage

Boundaries in Marriage, Dr. Henry Cloud and Dr. John Townsend

Children Change a Marriage, Elisa Morgan and Carol Kuykendall

Getting the Love You Want, Harville Hendrix

The Language of Love, Gary Smalley and John Trent

Men Are from Mars, Women Are from Venus, John Gray

Men Are Like Waffles, Women Are Like Spaghetti, Bill Farrel and Pam Farrel

The Power of a Praying Wife, Stormie Omartian

Ten Great Dates to Revitalize Your Marriage, David Arp and Claudia Arp

The Triumphant Marriage, Neil Clark Warren

Unbelieving Husbands and the Wives Who Love Them, Michael Fanstone

When He Doesn't Believe, Nancy Kennedy

Men and Fathering

Always Daddy's Girl, H. Norman Wright

Beside Every Great Dad, Nancy L. Swihart and Ken R. Canfield

Dear Dad, Doug Webster

The Father Book, Frank Minirth, Brian Newman, and Paul Warren

Fatherhood, Bill Cosby

Real Boys, William Pollack

The Seven Secrets of Effective Fathers, Ken R. Canfield

She Calls Me Daddy, Robert Wolgemuth

She's Had a Baby: And I'm Having a Meltdown, James Douglas Barron

199

What Husbands Wish Their Wives Knew about Men, Patrick
   M. Morley
What Kids Need in a Dad, Tim Hansel
Women Are Always Right and Men Are Never Wrong, Joey
   O'Connor

Women and Mothering

Boundaries, Dr. Henry Cloud and Dr. John Townsend
Brave Hearts, Sharon Hersh
The Eight Seasons of Parenthood, Barbara Unell and Jerry
   Wyckoff, Ph.D.
Imperfect Control, Judith Viorst
Mama's Little Baby, Dennis Brown and Pamela Tousaint
The Mom Factor, Dr. Henry Cloud and Dr. John Townsend
The Mother Dance: How Children Change Your Life, Harriet
   Lerner, Ph.D.
The Power of Mother Love, Brenda Hunter
What Every Child Needs, Elisa Morgan and Carol Kuykendall
What Every Mom Needs, Elisa Morgan and Carol Kuykendall

Parenting

Be There! John Trent
Boundaries with Kids, Dr. Henry Cloud and Dr. John
   Townsend
The New Hide and Seek, Dr. James Dobson
The Parent Survival Guide, Dr. Todd Cartmell
Raising Great Kids, Dr. Henry Cloud and Dr. John
   Townsend

Single Parenting

*Mom's House, Dad's House: Complete Guide for Parents Who
   Are Separated, Divorced or Remarried,* Isolina Ricci,
   Ph.D.

Moving On after He Moves Out, Jim Conway, Ph.D. and Sally
   Conway, M.S.
Parenting on Your Own, Dr. Lynda Hunter
Single Again: The Uncertain Journey, Jim Smoke
Successful Single Parenting: Going It Alone (group workbook
   and video), Gary Richmond

Recovery classes offered nationwide at
   www.DivorceCare.com

Notes

About This Book

1. Nancy L. Swihart and Ken R. Canfield, *Beside Every Great Dad* (Wheaton: Tyndale, 1993), 4.

chapter one: The Birth of a Father

1. Dave Barry, "Sadly Lacking Breasts, Dad's Role Is Doodie Duty," *Miami Herald* (May 7, 2000).
2. Dennis Brown and Pamela Tousaint, *Mama's Little Baby* (New York: Penguin Putnam, 1998), 250.
3. Ian Davis, *My Boys Can Swim! The Official Guide to Pregnancy*, quoted by Darryl E. Owens, *Orlando Sentinel,* in "Maternal Links," *Daily Camera* (September 18, 2000): 4B.
4. Nancy L. Swihart and Ken R. Canfield, *Beside Every Great Dad* (Wheaton: Tyndale, 1993), 6.
5. Barbara Unell and Jerry Wyckoff, *The Eight Seasons of Parenthood* (New York: Random House, 2000), 38.

6. Dr. Frank Minirth, Dr. Brian Newman, and Dr. Paul Warren, *The Father Book* (Nashville: Thomas Nelson, 1992), 11.

7. James Douglas Barron, *She's Had a Baby: I'm Having a Meltdown* (New York: Quill William Morrow, 1999), xiii–xiv.

8. Robert Byron, *Parents Say the Darndest Things,* quoted in *Peanut Butter Kisses and Mud Pie Hugs,* by Becky Freeman (Eugene, Ore.: Harvest House, 2000), 71.

9. "Al Roker on Weathering Fatherhood," *Daily Camera* (June 9, 2000).

10. Barron, *She's Had a Baby,* 5–6.

chapter two: Daddy Daze

1. Ken R. Canfield, *The Seven Secrets of Effective Fathers* (Wheaton: Tyndale, 1992), 7.

2. Dr. Frank Minirth, Dr. Brian Newman, and Dr. Paul Warren, *The Father Book* (Nashville: Thomas Nelson, 1992), 12.

3. Sara McLanahan and Karen Booth, "Mother-Only Families: Problems, Prospects, and Politics," *Journal of Marriage and the Family* 51 (1989): 557–80.

4. Kristen Nelson, "Dads Add," *Psychology Today* (November/ December 1999): 21.

5. Gary Oliver, "The War on Boys," *New Man* (November/ December 2000): 47–50ff., condensed in "Build a Generation of Godly Young Men," *Current Thoughts and Trends* (January 2001): 15.

6. Janet Simons, "Man to Man," *Denver Rocky Mountain News* (March 20, 2000): 3D, reviewing a book by Michael Gurlan, *The Wonder of Boys.*

7. Paul Vitz, *Faith of the Fatherless* (Dallas: Spence Publishing, 1999), 15–16.

8. Leonard Pitts, "Trashing Old Dad Gets a New Salute," *Denver Post* (February 22, 2001): 7B.

9. Erich Fromm as quoted by Philip Yancey in *The Jesus I Never Knew* (Grand Rapids: Zondervan, 1995), 158.

10. Jeff Dietz, "A Weekend Away," *MomSense* (April/May 2001): 12.

11. Minirth, Newman, and Warren, *The Father Book,* 12.

12. Patrick M. Morley, *What Husbands Wish Their Wives Knew about Men* (Grand Rapids: Zondervan, 1998), 184–85.

13. Ken R. Canfield, National Center for Fathering, "Promise Keepers' Sample 1995 National Survey of Men, Report on 1995 Conference Attendees."

14. Canfield, *Seven Secrets of Effective Fathers*, 4.

15. William Pollack, Ph.D., *Real Boys* (New York: Henry Holt, 1998), 127.

16. Dennis Brown and Pamela Tousaint, *Mama's Little Baby* (New York: Penguin Putnam, 1998), 245.

17. Mary Beth Grover, "Daddy Stress," *Forbes* (September 6, 1999): 202.

18. Judith Newman, "Dad Has His Day," *Ladies Home Journal* (October 2000): 21.

19. Suzanne Braun Levine, "The Good Daddy," *Ladies Home Journal* (April 2000): 98. Taken from *Father Courage: What Happens When Men Put Families First* (Harcourt, 2000).

20. Grover, "Daddy Stress," 208.

chapter three: A Mom's Job: In the Beginning and Beyond

1. Theresa Meyers quoted in *A Love Like No Other*, Elisa Morgan, ed. (Sisters, Ore: Multnomah, 2002), 9.

2. John Bowlby, *Attachment*, vol. 1, *Attachment and Loss* (New York: Basic Books, 1969), xi.

3. Deborah Shaw Lewis and Charmaine Crouse Yoest, *Mother in the Middle* (Grand Rapids: Zondervan, 1996), 92–93.

4. Sharon Begley, "Your Child's Brain," *Newsweek* (February 19, 1996): 55–61.

5. Dr. Henry Cloud and Dr. John Townsend, *Raising Great Kids* (Grand Rapids: Zondervan, 1999), 71.

6. Sigmund Freud, *Outline of Psychoanalysis SE 23* (London: Hogarth Press, 1940), 188.

7. John Bowlby, *Separation: Anxiety and Anger*, vol. 2, *Attachment and Loss* (New York: Basic Books, 1973), 204.

8. Cloud and Townsend, *Raising Great Kids*, 69.

9. Judith Viorst, *Imperfect Control* (New York: Simon and Schuster, 1998), 164.
10. Michael E. Lamb, "The Development of Mother-Infant and Father-Infant Attachment in the Second Year of Life," *Developmental Psychology* 13 (1977): 637–48; and Alan Sroufe and Everett Waters, "Attachment as an Organizational Construct," *Child Development* 48 (1977): 1186.
11. Dr. Henry Cloud and Dr. John Townsend, as quoted in a telephone interview with the authors, February 15, 2001.
12. James Douglas Barron, *She's Had a Baby: And I'm Having a Meltdown* (New York: Quill William Morrow, 1999), 22.
13. Brenda Hunter, *The Power of Mother Love* (Colorado Springs: WaterBrook, 1997), 108.
14. Lewis and Yoest, *Mother in the Middle,* 92–93.
15. Cloud and Townsend, *Raising Great Kids,* 77.
16. Armin A. Brott and Jennifer Ash, *The Expectant Father* (New York: Abbeville Press, 1995), 167.

chapter four: Heart Longings

1. Sharon A. Hersh, *Brave Hearts* (Colorado Springs: WaterBrook, 2000), 17, 22.
2. Dr. John Townsend, *Hiding from Love* (Colorado Springs: NavPress, 1991), 34.
3. Vicki Iovine, *The Girlfriends' Guide to Surviving the First Year of Motherhood* (New York: Berkley Publishing Group, 1997), 71.
4. Chrisy Hoss, "Caregiver or Caretaker," *MomSense* (July/August 1999): 7.
5. Dr. Henry Cloud and Dr. John Townsend, *The Mom Factor* (Grand Rapids: Zondervan, 1996), 227.
6. Iovine, *Girlfriends' Guide,* 71.

chapter five: Mind Warps

1. Dr. Frank Minirth, Dr. Brian Newman, and Dr. Paul Warren, *The Father Book* (Nashville: Thomas Nelson, 1992), 28.
2. Richard Weissbourd, "Distancing Dad," *American Prospect* (December 6, 1999, vol. 11, no. 2): 32–34, condensed in "To Get

Dads Involved," *Current Thoughts and Trends* (February 2000): 10–11.

3. Armin A. Brott and Jennifer Ash, *The Expectant Father* (New York: Abbeville Press, 1995), 194.

4. Judith Viorst, *Imperfect Control* (New York: Simon and Schuster, 1998), 42.

5. Ibid., 55.

6. Brott and Ash, *Expectant Father,* 195.

7. Nancy L. Swihart and Ken R. Canfield, *Beside Every Great Dad* (Wheaton: Tyndale, 1993), 10.

chapter six: A Mom's Choice: Puppet or Partner?

1. Richard Weissbourd, "Distancing Dad," *American Prospect* (December 6, 1999, vol. 11, no. 2): 32–34, condensed in "To Get Dads Involved," *Current Thoughts and Trends* (February 2000): 10.

2. Dr. Henry Cloud and Dr. John Townsend, *Boundaries* (Grand Rapids: Zondervan, 1992), 29.

3. Ibid., 30–31.

4. Nancy L. Swihart and Ken R. Canfield, *Beside Every Great Dad* (Wheaton: Tyndale, 1993), 10.

5. Ruth Barton, *Becoming a Woman of Strength* (Wheaton: Shaw, 1994), 193.

6. Tara Parker-Pope and Kyle Pope, "A Balanced Life: Women Pay a Price for Control," *Wall Street Journal Sunday* (November 19, 2000): 2.

7. William Pollack, Ph.D., *Real Boys* (New York: Henry Holt, 1998), 125.

8. Becky Freeman, *Marriage 911* (Nashville: Broadman and Holman, 1996), 32.

9. Elisa Morgan and Carol Kuykendall, *Children Change a Marriage* (Grand Rapids: Zondervan, 1999), 178–81.

10. Barton, *Becoming a Woman of Strength,* 205.

11. Neil Clark Warren, Ph.D., *Learning to Live with the Love of Your Life and Loving It,* previously titled *The Triumphant Marriage* (Colorado Springs: Focus on the Family, 1995), 141.

chapter seven: He's Not "Duh," He's Different

1. Leonard Pitts, "Trashing Old Dad Gets a New Salute," *Denver Post* (February 22, 2001): 7B.

2. Bill Farrel and Pam Farrel, *Men Are Like Waffles; Women Are Like Spaghetti* (Eugene, Ore.: Harvest House, 2001), 11–16.

3. "Worst Joke of the Week," *Daily Camera* (August 27, 2000).

4. Dr. Benjamin Spock as quoted in Buzz McClain, "The Father Files," *Colorado Parent* (June 1999): 23.

5. Patricia Clancy Kiefner, "Letting Go and Letting Dad," *Welcome Home* (August 2000): 6.

6. Wade Horn, quoted by Don Eberly, ed., *The Faith Factor in Fatherhood*, reviewed in *Current Thoughts and Trends* (June 2000): 13–14.

7. Robert B. McCall, "The Importance of Fathers," *Parents* (August 1980): 82.

8. Al Roker as interviewed by Barbara Kantrowitz in "This Father Knows Best," *Newsweek* Special Issue (fall/winter 2000): 68.

9. Joey O'Connor, *Women Are Always Right and Men Are Never Wrong* (Nashville: Word, 1998), 205.

10. Amitai Etzioni, as quoted in "Dan Quayle Was Right," *Atlantic Monthly Article*, digital edition (April 1993): 19.

chapter eight: Understanding Original Differences

1. Judith Viorst, *Necessary Losses* (New York: Simon and Schuster, 1986), 192.

2. H. Norman Wright, *Always Daddy's Girl: Understanding Your Father's Impact on Who You Are* (Ventura, Calif.: Regal, 1989), 10.

3. Wright, *Always Daddy's Girl*, 14–21.

4. Brenda Hunter, *Home by Choice* (Portland, Ore.: Multnomah, 1991), 185.

5. William Pollack, Ph.D., *Real Boys* (New York: Henry Holt, 1998), 81.

6. Dr. Frank Minirth, Dr. Brian Newman, and Dr. Paul Warren, *The Father Book* (Nashville: Thomas Nelson, 1992), 30–32.

chapter nine: Dealing with the Differences

1. Judith Viorst, *Imperfect Control* (New York: Simon and Schuster, 1998), 57.
2. Nancy L. Swihart and Ken R. Canfield, *Beside Every Great Dad* (Wheaton: Tyndale, 1993), 92.
3. Ken Canfield, *The Seven Secrets of Effective Fathers* (Wheaton: Tyndale, 1992), 7.
4. Dennis Brown and Pamela Tousaint, *Mama's Little Baby* (New York: Penguin Putnam, 1998), 250, 253.
5. Swihart and Canfield, *Beside Every Great Dad,* 78.
6. Patrick M. Morley, *What Husbands Wish Their Wives Knew about Men* (Grand Rapids: Zondervan, 1998), 208–9.

chapter ten: Let Dad Be Dad

1. Nancy L. Swihart and Ken R. Canfield, *Beside Every Great Dad* (Wheaton: Tyndale, 1993), 91–92.
2. Ken Canfield, *The Seven Secrets of Effective Fathers* (Wheaton: Tyndale, 1992), 193.
3. Ken Canfield, "Welcome to Dad's World," *Christian Parenting Today* (March/April 2000): 36.
4. Paul C. Vitz, *Faith of the Fatherless,* (Dallas: Spence Publishing, 1999), 16.
5. Canfield, *Seven Secrets of Effective Fathers,* 174–75; Cynthia Clark, "The Transmission of Religious Beliefs and Practices for Parents to Firstborn Early Adolescent Sons," *Journal of Marriage and the Family* 50 (May 1988): 463–72.
6. Steve Schlissel, "Make Room for Daddies," *Chalcedon Report* (March 2000, Issue 416): 8–17.
7. Canfield, *Seven Secrets of Effective Fathers,* 174.
8. Stormie Omartian, *The Power of a Praying Wife* (Eugene, Ore.: Harvest House, 1997), 13.
9. Swihart and Canfield, *Beside Every Great Dad,* 158.
10. Ibid., 10.

Summing It Up: Mommy and Daddy Style

1. Jeff Dietz, "A Weekend Away," *MomSense* (April/May 2001): 12.

What to Do Next

1. Adapted from Patrick M. Morley, *What Husbands Wish Their Wives Knew about Men* (Grand Rapids: Zondervan, 1998), 212–17.

2. Elisa Morgan, *God's Words of Life for Moms* (Grand Rapids: Zondervan, 2000), 17.

3. Elisa Morgan and Carol Kuykendall, *What Every Mom Needs* (Grand Rapids: Zondervan, 1995), 68.

4. Ibid., 70.

5. Adapted from Patricia H. Sprinkle, *Children Who Do Too Little* (Grand Rapids: Zondervan, 1996), 87.

6. Morgan and Kuykendall, *What Every Mom Needs,* 124.

7. Ibid., 131–32.

8. Adapted from Armin A. Brott and Jennifer Ash, *The Expectant Father* (New York: Abbeville Press, 1995), 195–98.

9. Adapted from William Pollack, *Real Boys* (New York: Henry Holt, 1998), 137–44.

10. Dr. Henry Cloud and Dr. John Townsend, *Safe People* (Grand Rapids: Zondervan, 1995), 166–67.

11. Based on *Psychology: Its Principles and Meanings,* 4th ed., by Lyle E. Bourne Jr., and Bruce R. Ekstrand (New York: Holt, Rinehart, and Winston, 1976), 298, 306, 308.

12. Charles R. Swindoll, *Wisdom for the Way* (Nashville: J. Countryman, 2001), 19.

13. Ibid., 339.

14. Sharon Randall, "How to Stay Married," *Daily Camera* (August 27, 2000): 6D.

15. Karen Scalf Linamen, *Pillow Talk: The Intimate Marriage from A to Z* (Grand Rapids: Revell, 1996), 89.

16. Elisa Morgan, "Wise Woman," *MomSense* (April/May 2001), 19.

17. By Luis Palau, excerpted from *NIV Starting Point Study Bible* (Grand Rapids: Zondervan, 2002).

18. Elisa Morgan and Carol Kuykendall, *When Husband and Wife Become Mom and Dad* (Grand Rapids: Zondervan, 1999), 174–76.

19. Adapted from Michael Fanstone, *Unbelieveing Husbands and the Wives Who Love Them* (Ann Arbor: Servant, 1994), 61–76.

20. Stormie Omartian, *The Power of a Praying Wife* (Eugene, Ore.: Harvest House, 1997), 138.
21. Ibid., 140–41.
22. Adapted from Nancy L. Swihart and Ken R. Canfield, *Beside Every Great Dad* (Wheaton: Tyndale, 1993), 271–79.

Credits

Baby Blues cartoon reprinted with special permission of King Features Syndicate.

Barron, James Douglas, *She's Had a Baby: And I'm Having a Meltdown.* Copyright © 1998 by James Douglas Barron. Reprinted by permission of HarperCollins Publishers Inc.

Barry, Dave, "Sadly Lacking Breasts, Dad's Role Is Doodie Duty." Used by permission. Dave Barry is a syndicated humor columnist with the *Miami Herald.*

Baumbich, Charlene Ann, "The Watermelon Picnic." Used with permission of the author.

Bourne, Lyle E. Jr., and Bruce R. Ekstrand, *Psychology: Its Principles and Meanings,* 4th ed. © 1982. Reprinted with permission of Wadsworth, an imprint of the Wadsworth Group, a division of Thomson Learning. Fax 800-730-2215.

Cantrell, Julie Perkins, "Daddy, Wait." Used with permission of the author.

Quick Topic Finder

Use this outline to quickly find topics covered in the section "What to Do Next."

The MOPS Story

MOPS stands for Mothers of Preschoolers, a program designed to encourage mothers with children under school age through relationships and resources. These women come from different backgrounds and lifestyles, yet have similar needs and a shared desire to be the best mothers they can be!

A MOPS group provides a caring, accepting atmosphere for today's mother of preschoolers. Here she has an opportunity to share concerns, explore areas of creativity, and hear instruction that equips her for the responsibilities of family and community. The MOPS group also includes MOPPETS, a loving, learning experience for children.

Approximately 2,700 groups meet in churches throughout the United States, Canada, and 19 other countries, to meet the needs of more than 100,000 women. Many more mothers are encouraged by MOPS resources, including *MOMSense* radio and magazine, MOPS' web site, and publications such as this book.

Find out how MOPS International can help you become part of the MOPS♥to♥Mom Connection.

MOPS International
P.O. Box 102200
Denver, CO 80250-2200
Phone 1-800-929-1287 or 303-733-5353
E-mail: Info@MOPS.org
Web site: http://www.MOPS.org

To learn how to start a MOPS group,
call 1-888-910-MOPS.
For MOPS products call The MOPShop
1-888-545-4040.

MOTHERS OF
M♥PS®
PRESCHOOLERS
...because mothering matters

What Every Mom Needs

Meet *Your* Nine Basic Needs
(and Be a Better Mom)

ELISA MORGAN
& CAROL KUYKENDALL

You'll love this best-selling book in which Elisa Morgan and Carol Kuykendall point the way to relief and fulfillment in the midst of motherhood's hectic pace. After more than twenty years of research and experience with moms, MOPS has identified your nine basic needs as a mother: significance, identity, growth, intimacy, instruction, help, recreation, perspective, and hope. *What Every Mom Needs* is an invaluable resource for women who long to expand their personal horizons and become better mothers at the same time.

Softcover 0-310-21920-5

Pick up a copy at your favorite bookstore today!

ZONDERVAN™

GRAND RAPIDS, MICHIGAN 49530

WWW.ZONDERVAN.COM

Children Change a Marriage
What Every Couple Needs

ELISA MORGAN
& CAROL KUYKENDALL

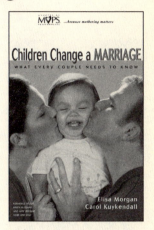

B ased on twenty-six years of experience with parents of preschoolers
and the results of 1,000 questionnaires
sent to new moms and dads, this book
helps you and your mate understand
and meet six areas of need in your
marriage:

> BALANCE—What's happened to our marriage?
> COMMITMENT—Will you love me even when it's
> hard?
> INTERDEPENDENCE—Who are you and me now
> that we are three?
> MISSION—What makes this family a family?
> HOPE—Where is "happily ever after?"

Like the whimsical mobile to which Morgan and
Kuykendall liken a marriage, you and your spouse will
inevitably wobble in your relationship when a baby throws
your two-person balance off kilter. But while regaining equi-
librium takes hard work, the payoffs are worth the effort.
Children Change a Marriage will inspire new vision for the
creative masterpiece your marriage can become when the two
of you enlarge into a family.

Softcover 0-310-24299-1

Pick up a copy today at your favorite bookstore!

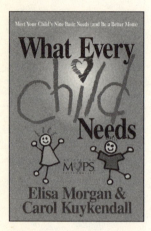

In the Wee Hours

Up-in-the-Nighttime Stories for Mom

COMPILED BY MARY BETH LAGERBORG

Selections from Ruth Bell Graham, Elisa Morgan, Elisabeth Elliott, Erma Bombeck, and many more!

Whether you're changing a diaper, comforting a toddler who's had a nightmare, or waiting up late for your teen to come home, being up at night isn't an option when you're a mom. It's a lifestyle.

Wouldn't it be wonderful to have a late-night companion to offer you encouragement, inspiration, even a chuckle or two? You've found one. Filled with humor, poetry, reflections, and poignant stories, all written by and about women, this collection is designed to chase away frustration and worry, and help you relax, laugh, hope, and dream.

Refresh yourself with selections by Valerie Bell, Erma Bombeck, Gloria Gaither, Carol Kuykendall, Anne Morrow Lindbergh, Elisa Morgan, Chonda Pierce, Anna Quindlen, Luci Shaw, Ingrid Trobisch, and others. Set this book by your favorite chair—and reach for it whenever you need a pick-me-up during those night watches.

Softcover 0-1-310-24024-7

Pick up a copy today at your favorite bookstore!

Little Books for Busy Moms

Softcover
0-310-23513-8

Time out for Mom ...Ahhh Moments
BUSY MOMS
MARY BETH LAGERBORG general editor
written by CYNTHIA W. SUMNER

Great Books to Read and Fun Things to Do with Them
BUSY MOMS
MARY BETH LAGERBORG general editor
written by JANE C. JARRELL

Softcover
0-310-23515-4

If you ever needed Friends, it's now
BUSY MOMS
MARY BETH LAGERBORG general editor
written by LESLIE PARROTT

Softcover
0-310-23514-6

Kids' stuff and What to Do with It
BUSY MOMS
MARY BETH LAGERBORG general editor
written by LEIGH ROLLAR MINTZ

Softcover
0-310-23511-1

Boredom Busters
BUSY MOMS
MARY BETH LAGERBORG general editor
written by BARBARA VOGELGESANG

Softcover
0-310-23997-4

Juggling Tasks, Tots, & Time
BUSY MOMS
MARY BETH LAGERBORG general editor
written by CATHY PENSHORN

Softcover
0-310-24178-2

Planes, Trains, & Automobiles ... with Kids!
BUSY MOMS
MARY BETH LAGERBORG general editor
written by CYNTHIA W. SUMNER

Softcover
0-310-23999-0